Student-Led Conferences

Using portfolios to share learning with parents

JANET MILLAR GRANT
BARBARA HEFFLER
KADRI MEREWEATHER

Pembroke Publishers Limited

To mom with love.
Janet

To my mother, Vivian Brown, with all my love.
Barbara

To my best friend Doug.
Kadri

538 Hood Road
Markham, Ontario
L3R 3K9

The *Student Growth Plan for Achieving Mastery* (page 94) is presented with the permission of the York Region Board of Education.

Canadian Cataloguing in Publication Data

Grant, Janet Millar, 1960-
Student-led conferences: using portfolios to share learning with parents

ISBN 1-55138-054-4

1. Parent-teacher conferences. 2. Teacher-student relationships. I. Heffler, Barbara. II. Mereweather, Kadri. III. Title.

LC225.5.G73 1995 372.11′03 C95-931607-8

A catalogue record for this book is available from the British Library.
Published in the U.K. by
Drake Educational Associates
St. Fagan's Road, Fairwater, Cardiff CF5 3A3

Editor: Kate Revington
Design: John Zehethofer
Cover Photography: Ajay Photographics
Typesetting: Jay Tee Graphics Ltd.

Printed and bound in Canada
9 8 7 6 5 4 3 2

Contents

Towards a Vision

We have discovered the tremendous potential of a process whereby the student assumes the responsibility for planning, implementing, conducting, and evaluating a conference with at least one parent present. It is called Student-Led Conferencing. Our discoveries have excited us so much that we want to share them with you. We have written this book to provide support and guidance for anyone taking a journey towards Student-Led Conferencing.

Common Concerns

All three of us on the writing team have worked with students in a variety of teaching environments and situations: mentoring, team teaching, teaching with an aide, providing in-class support, as subject specialists, as homeroom teachers, teaching in an open concept situation, and teaching on a rotary timetable among them. During these experiences questions and concerns about assessment and evaluation and reporting to parents arose.

As curriculum consultants working with teachers to develop curriculum, we found more questions than answers about assessment and evaluation. These questions held true despite a wide range in subject areas and a span from preschool to post-secondary education. We decided to address our common questions through research.

Our main concern centred on the effectiveness of the traditional parent-teacher interview as a method of communicating student learning. We felt that no matter how successful traditional interviews were, there had to be a better way! In this belief we began researching alternative forms of reporting to parents. Information on Student-Led Conferencing intrigued us so we decided to investigate and explore the concept further with the help of three pilot classes in the York Region Board of Education, Ontario. The three pilot teachers are Kevin Doran, Krista Walford, and Sally Landy, and they teach Grades 3, 5/6, and 7/8 respectively.

Assessing the Parent-Teacher Interview

Our explorations began with an assessment of the traditional parent-teacher interview.

When parents enter the classroom for such an interview, they revisit their past. They become the students once again and see the teacher as the authority figure. Parents are often at a disadvantage because they don't know what to expect. Sometimes, teachers use educational jargon which can distance parents. The first language of parents may not be the language of the interview, as is the case for some recent immigrant families or for those with children at French Immersion schools. This may cause parents to feel even more out of place in the school environment.

The level of parental nervousness surprised us. In our classroom teaching days, we spent much time reassuring parents that their children were doing just fine. Most parents did not know what questions to ask. That meant we had to take on even more ownership and direction of the conference. Perhaps our greatest problem was communicating with those parents for whom English was not a first language. And those parents most needed to hear and react to reports being, in many cases, totally unfamiliar with the curriculum, program delivery and focus of the school programs.

As well-educated professionals, we assumed that a parent-teacher interview in which one of us was the parent would be comfortable. Surprisingly, Janet found that she was very nervous sitting on the other side of a desk. She came to the conference prepared with questions she wanted answered. However, she was so intent on interpreting the information and "reading between the lines" that she ended up leaving the conference without the desired answers. Imagine how unsatisfied parents must feel if they aren't in the "educational field."

Our past experiences told us that the number of parents attending parent-teacher interviews decreased as the grade increased. In early primary grades, we found that parents attended every parent-teacher interview and indeed any school function. In the middle years, as students asserted their independence, they often did not take notes home. Effective communication became more difficult. By the time students reached high school, we would be lucky if five percent of the parents attended a parent-teacher interview.

During informal interview nights, most elementary school teachers find themselves dealing with about thirty sets of parents within a two-hour time frame. Dealing effectively with all of the questions and issues about student learning is physically and emotionally impossible. These meet-the-teacher nights occur within the first six weeks of school, at which time teachers are still assessing students and are somewhat reluctant to make evaluative judgments on students' academic achievements. Some discussion about how students are doing does take place, however.

We found that those attending the traditional end-of-term parent-teacher interviews, optional in our board, were usually the parents of successful students or those who had been specifically requested to attend. The latter were hard to contact and reluctant to come; they knew they would hear negative comments about their child's truancy, poor performance or inappropriate behavior. The overall experience left us with several questions to pursue, including "Is there a clear focus for the interview?" and "What impact will it have on student learning?"

Every year we gathered work samples, documented descriptions of student progress, and then planned and delivered this information on student achievement to parents in an interview.

As "directors" of the parent-teacher interviews we found it difficult to involve parents meaningfully. After conducting one, identifying student strengths, needs, and interventions, we would enlist parental support for working at home with their child. But most parents are now employed outside the home. Finding time to provide this support is difficult. Sometimes, parents feel that teaching is the teacher's job only, and that they don't have time for any of it. All the same, we wondered what effective supporting role parents might take.

Surely there was something better than what was normally done . . .

Increasing Student Involvement

The traditional parental role has been to help the child with projects and reteach those things that the child had difficulty with in class.

Essentially, parents tutored their child without having any training in current educational practices. They received little direction as to what their supporting role would be.

Parental nervousness arises due to several reasons. We often overlook the fact that parents are a child's first teacher and can still contribute to their learning. They may perceive that their child's performance in school reflects directly on them. Some parents only attend interviews when concerns about student performance and behavior surface. As a result, parents may see an interview as an adversarial or confrontational situation, not as a forum for sharing information.

To counterbalance that, in part, we looked at different ways of involving students. First students served as tour guides for visiting parents and other guests. In this role, they led parents around the school, hallways and classrooms, answering questions and offering information about school activities. We received positive feedback from those parents and guests. Their comments reflected the pride, confidence and ownership demonstrated by the students.

As the students experienced small successes, we increased their involvement with and ownership of conferences with parents. For the first informal parent and teacher meeting of the year, we explored possible ways of incorporating students as "representers" of their own learning. Students played a part in the meeting, presenting, discussing, and working through work samples and activities.

During such a curriculum night students proudly led their families into and around the classroom, and discussed their learning experiences, their contributions to class bulletin boards and activities, and their progress in identified subject areas as evidenced through their workbooks. Finally, students introduced their parents to the classroom teacher. Parents then had an opportunity to informally discuss general issues pertaining to their child. With this structure announced in advance, parents turned out in record numbers. It was wonderful to see the pride and confidence of the students and the interest and involvement in classroom activities of the families. The student contribution on this evening allowed teachers the time to meet with each family and address particular questions and concerns about the class program.

Since teachers still found that they needed help communicating student learning to parents, they turned, quite reasonably, to their students. They used class time to help students identify what they knew, what they needed to know and how they would go about learning it. They provided lessons on communicating with others in role-playing situations, and modeled the discussion of student work samples and what learning was demonstrated in those samples. By so doing they were able to prepare students in a small way to represent their own learning. Students became responsible for it.

Supporting Student Learning

It was at this time that we began to question and refocus our own thoughts on interviews and conferencing. We made the shift from looking at the negative aspects of student learning to the positive and how we could support their continued learning. Current trends in education have changed the way we look at learning. Where students were once viewed as empty vessels to be filled, educators now believe that students need to know what learning is and what it looks like. In the past, learning was content driven; today the focus is on the learning process.

The work of Howard Gardner in *Frames of Mind* has made us realize that learning is far more complex than we had previously thought. Learning happens in a variety of ways and through a variety of intelligences. We all have the seven intelligences in varying degrees, but traditional schools have valued some more than others.

1. Linguistic Intelligence:	"The capacity to use words effectively, whether orally . . . or in writing . . ."
2. Logical-Mathematical Intelligence:	"The capacity to use numbers effectively . . . and to reason well . . ."
3. Spatial Intelligence:	"The ability to perceive the visual-spatial world accurately . . . and to perform transformations upon those perceptions . . ."
4. Bodily-Kinesthetic Intelligence:	"Expertise in using one's whole body to express ideas and feelings . . . and facility in using one's hands to produce or transform things . . ."
5. Musical Intelligence:	"The capacity to perceive . . . , discriminate . . . , transform . . . , and express . . . musical forms."
6. Interpersonal Intelligence:	"The ability to perceive and make distinctions in the moods, intentions, motivations, and feelings of other people."
7. Intrapersonal Intelligence:	"Self-knowledge and the ability to act adaptively on the basis of that knowledge."

Adapted from Thomas Armstrong's *Multiple Intelligences in the Classroom*

We expect that in schools of the future, the intelligences that have been less highly valued, such as the ability to reflect on one's own learning (intrapersonal), will become vital. Thomas Armstrong in *Multiple Intelligences in the Classroom* states that "this intelligence includes having an accurate picture of oneself (one's strengths and limitations): awareness of inner moods, intentions, motivations, temperaments and desires, and the capacity for self-discipline, self-understanding, and self-esteem." These reflective skills are critical to the success of portfolios and conferencing which we will be discussing further in this book.

If we want to showcase students to their best advantage, we need to make sure that our classroom programs will provide learning experiences that draw on all of the seven intelligences. If we do that, then every child will have a chance for success.

Students Present at Conferences

One of our writing team first became involved with having students at parent conferences as a result of a parent's babysitting dilemma. That parent requested that the student be present. This request caused the teacher to reflect on whether or not she had to see the parent privately. The answer was no. The teacher then found that having the child at the conference provided all members with an opportunity for input and allowed everyone to hear the same message. The teacher no longer had to justify her evaluation of that child by herself since the child could answer any questions or address concerns.

After further investigation we realized there wasn't anything any one of us had to say about a student that could not be said in front of the student. Marks and anecdotals should be shared with students on an individual basis, but, of course, class lists of marks should not. Each teacher on the research team agreed that they had to be up front and honest with all students, regardless of the grade level, so that students could fully know their strengths and areas for improvement. If any major concern about a student arose, we would communicate that to both the student and the parents well in advance of any conference.

We found that such a conference provides a tremendous source of background information on the child, a snapshot of the interactions and relationships in the home and the "social/emotional baggage" that the child brings to school.

We began to be more systematic. As a research team of educators, each with unique past classroom experiences, we spent the first few months of each year providing direct instruction with many opportunities for clear feedback on student performance. As often as possible, we tried to give each student feedback about his or her development and progress. We would compare a student's work to past work samples and discuss what learning the samples gave evidence of. Care was taken to provide appropriate goals for the student as well as to discuss the strategies which would be used to achieve those goals.

Many teachers tried Three-Way Conferences with varying degrees of success. One example of a Three-Way Conference took place between Matthew, his parents, and his teacher.

> They sat around a table with Matthew's work books and collected work samples and discussed his progress. The teacher conducted the conference by predetermining the areas and issues to cover, and Matthew did the majority of work sample presentation and much of the talking. What was fascinating was the respect and honest communication that took place between parent and child. The parents were quick to discuss ways that they could offer support.

It certainly reinforced the teacher's classroom philosophy of involving students in their learning while inviting parental involvement with and commitment to the learning process.

There you have it, our beginnings. After the Three-Way Conference there was no turning back. We had found that in the traditional format students have little academic direction for their studies beyond the completion of assigned work. We had experienced difficulty motivating some students. They had no sense of their own progress and were often looking for reasons why they had to do an assigned task. Such students are difficult to motivate and reluctant to carry through a task, to be responsible and to commit to their school work. The Three-Way Conference resulted in improved student attitudes, behaviors, and learning. We knew we were on the right path.

The Potential for Greater Student Participation

Once we had experienced this success with Three-Way Conferencing, we saw even more potential for student involvement through Student-Led Conferencing.

We developed a vision of what Student-Led Conferencing could be: students comfortable and familiar with their own progress, learning what they find meaningful, and having identified knowledge, skills and attitudes; students at the centre of the process with their parents, a process that calls upon all participants to communicate commitment and support for lifelong learning.

In our vision, every parent attends a Student-Led Conference. Here, parents would hear about the educational program in an understandable way and show support for and learn more about their children's academic progress. Parents are welcomed by their children and draw comfort from their confident presence. They readily talk with their children, even in a first language other than English, listen to them describe their learning, and discuss and set goals with them to address weaknesses and areas for growth.

We are convinced that Student-Led Conferencing is the best way to communicate student learning regardless of the age or grade of the child.

One teacher who has pursued our vision has made Student-Led Conferencing an integral part of her daily program with tremendous results. She began with a math portfolio and specific learning outcomes. The students developed portfolios, choosing the learning outcomes to be addressed and deciding how they would achieve success. They felt they were in charge of their learning. "It was theirs and they were proud of it." They demonstrated this ownership during the Student-Led Conferences with their parents.

These students have learned how to set goals and monitor their own growth. When asked what they would change about the process of Student-Led Conferencing, they unanimously declared, "It's perfect, don't change a thing!" The teacher sees Student-Led Conferencing as "a gift from heaven." Bearing in mind that none of them have been involved in Student-Led Conferencing before, there are some wrinkles to be ironed out, but overall they couldn't be more committed to the process (Maureen Wilkinson's Grade 5 class, York Region Board of Education, Ontario).

Kevin Doran, Sally Landy and Krista Walford have all set out to implement Student-Led Conferencing in the classroom. Once other teachers in our system heard about it, they became involved with the process and contributed to our findings. All of us meet regularly to discuss and support one another toward our vision of

Student-Led Conferencing. Everyone in the pilot continues to be amazed and excited by what has taken place. This excitement is contagious, and is spreading to other teachers who are joining our research team in pursuit of this vision.

Realizing it takes time. Although you can leap directly into Student-Led Conferencing, you may be wise to ease into it through Three-Way Conferences. And successful Student-Led Conferencing requires a substantial investment of time: time for preparation, time for the actual conferences, and time for debriefing.

"Yes, it does take a lot of time," said one teacher, but then went on to conclude, "The payoff is 100 percent worth it!"

1. Educating for the Future

> The old Chinese proverb that questions whether it is better to give a man a fish for today or teach him the art of fishing to prepare him for a lifetime applies quite well to the contemporary task of education . . .
>
> — David Lazear, *Seven Ways of Teaching*

The Underlying Challenge

Restructuring initiatives in education have spread all across North America in a quest to address the issues of accountability and improved student learning. The key question that individuals are asking is, "Are we preparing our students for the twenty-first century?"

Traditionally, students could rely on the labor industry for employment. In 1950, an incomplete high school education would still allow you to get a job in the unskilled job market. In the 1990s, the availability of such jobs has dropped dramatically. In the Information Age many of these jobs are now mechanized and/or computerized, thus decreasing the need for unskilled labor. This age requires workers to be both computer literate and able to learn new technology.

If you look at the composition of our work force, you can notice a drastic change from fifty years ago. Currently, professionals make up 20 percent of the work force and this number is increasing. In the past if you were trained for a specific job, you could probably keep that job until retirement. But no longer. "Scientific knowledge has been growing exponentially by some estimates doubling every six to ten years since the 1960s" (*Fortune*, May 1993). Because of this fact, students will need to adapt to change quickly and effectively, changing and retraining for several jobs over the course of their work careers. *If students learn how to learn, they will be able to make the necessary transitions, to become self-directed, lifelong learners.*

When parents and professionals are asked, "What do you want your child to know, do and value when they leave school?" the issues that arise, other than literacy and numeracy, are not of content but rather of life skills. The Conference Board of Canada's *Employability Skills Profile* (1992) lists critical skills that the business community believes are needed for the future job market. These "broad functional" skills are also life skills, skills required of a contributing and responsible citizen. The critical skills required of the future work force will include academic skills (those used in communicating, thinking and learning), personal management skills (a sense of responsibility, adaptability, the willingness to take initiative), and teamwork skills (the ability to work with others). The relative importance of teamwork in the future is interesting to note.

As jobs change, the structure of the educational system will have to adapt. But we don't know what the jobs of the future will be, so how do we train students for them? Workers will need to think independently, work as part of a team, and be innovative rather than just industrious. One aspect that we have not encouraged enough in schools is the development of entrepreneurial skills. As self-starters, entrepreneurs create their own jobs to meet society's needs. We can provide students with a body of transferable skills that would enable them to adapt to any new job requirement. What we want to focus on is the process of how to learn and how to access the information necessary to meet future challenges.

Two views about the purpose of education are converging. Many feel that the purpose of education is to produce well-rounded students who are lifelong, self-directed learners and contributing and responsible members of an ever-changing society. As well, some have always felt that the purpose of education was to train and prepare students for employment or entrepreneurial roles. The result is a common purpose for education: to produce students who are lifelong, self-directed learners with the necessary skills to contribute to society and meet the demands of future jobs.

As the skill requirements for future jobs change, students will have to show prospective employers — or clients, if they become entrepreneurs — not only what they know, do and value but also that they can adapt to change. The application process will shift from an emphasis on a résumé, which lists education and past work experience, to a portfolio, which provides authentic evidence of an applicant's ability to perform the job successfully. A résumé might indicate that the applicant has taken four computer courses, while a portfolio would contain a piece of evidence to demonstrate what the applicant has learned to do on the computer.

The Changing Emphasis of Assessment and Evaluation

The purpose of assessment and evaluation is to support and improve learning. Assessment and evaluation are integral components of education. As we grow and change, our educational system must align assessment and evaluation practices to reflect that change.

The terms "assessment" and "evaluation" are often used interchangeably, but they mean two different things. **Assessment** is the ongoing collection of data, including written work, teacher observations, group work and student reflections; **evaluation** is a judgment based upon the assessment instruments. In mathematics, for example, the assessment could involve the collection and consideration of daily exercises and drills, while the evaluation would be a judgment based on an end-of-unit test or demonstration.

A strong and obvious connection must exist between the learning process and the methods of assessment. In the past the assessment emphasis led students to conclude that the learning of facts was the most important component of education. That focus no longer stands up.

Today we want to produce self-motivated, self-directed lifelong learners by having students begin to examine their learning critically. As they become more involved in their own learning, they become increasingly motivated and are able to set goals and monitor their own progress. Who knows better about a student's learning than that student? If they use self-reflection and self-assessment honestly, students do become accountable for their own learning.

Authentic Assessment

To truly reflect student learning, we need authentic assessment instruments. **Authentic** pertains to real-life experiences or demonstrations as opposed to pencil-and-paper tests or evaluation by invisible criteria. An authentic assessment instrument would apply the knowledge and skills to a real-life situation, for example, a class project to raise money to support a foster child in a Third World country. In this instance students needed to develop a plan to raise funds. They decided to sell popcorn. They had to calculate the costs of the bags, the oil, and the popcorn to determine the profit margin. They determined how many bags they needed to sell in order to support the child for the upcoming year. This exercise was successful because students could see the validity and purpose behind it.

> A move toward more authentic tasks and outcomes thus improves teaching and learning: students have greater clarity about their obligations (and are asked to master more engaging tasks) . . . teachers can come to believe that assessment results are both meaningful and useful in improving instruction.
>
> — Grant Wiggins, Workshop 1990

One of the best examples of authentic assessment is a student-prepared portfolio. Through it students identify and articulate accumulated skills and abilities, and can share information about them with their parents. The perfect vehicle for this sharing is a Student-Led Conference, which works at *any* grade level. In such a conference, the student takes his or her learning beyond the classroom walls, thereby simulating a "real-life" presentation, and the parents support the child.

Portfolios are not just for conferencing with parents. Entrance into secondary and post-secondary education may require them. A high school of the performing arts would probably require a portfolio that demonstrates the student's level of skill prior to admission to its programs. Admission to a journalism program may depend upon the presentation of a portfolio of the student's writing. Even now, students are asked to present portfolios for part- or full-time employment.

As a result of research and observation, educators now know more about how children learn. We know that we need to include real-life, purposeful experiences in their education, where they have ownership and choices.

Authentic Learning

Student performance has shown that the link between classroom practice and the real world is important for student motivation and ownership. Relevance is the key to learning. How many times have we heard students say, "This is boring — who cares what happened in 1600?"? James Beane, the well-known American middle school educator and author, believes that authentic learning involves negotiating rather than dictating curriculum and that students must identify questions that they want answered instead of our stipulating what they must learn. The themes and concerns of the curriculum, based upon provincial or state requirements, should be negotiated between student and teacher, to identify what we are going to do and how we are going to do it. The result of this student-centred learning is that students are motivated and take ownership within relevant curriculum. Someone needs to facilitate and guide students through this process. In student-centred learning, the teacher acts as a facilitator rather than as the source of all knowledge.

The teacher of the future will facilitate the communication between school and home about student progress. The word "facilitate" often has a negative connotation to parents. They perceive facilitation as being unstructured and not really teaching; however, even as facilitators, teachers still teach lessons and skills.

The vehicle through which such communication can best be shared is a Student-Led Conference centred on a portfolio of student work. Students have traditionally conferenced with teachers and peers about their school work, but that information has not always been shared with parents. **Student-Led Conferencing**, as outlined in this book, refers to the process whereby the student plans, implements, conducts and evaluates a conference. It provides a forum in which students can effectively talk about their school work with parents. It will allow them to celebrate their growth towards being self-directed, lifelong learners.

2. Types of Conferences

conference: a meeting of two or more persons for discussing matters of common concern.

— *Merriam-Webster's Collegiate Dictionary, Tenth Edition*

As classroom teachers, we consider a conference to be a discussion centred around a child's learning. The purpose of the conference and the past reporting experiences of students and parents determine how conferences should be approached. Depending on the purpose, the participants will change and may be any combination of students, parents, and teachers.

Peer Conference

A peer conference occurs anytime two or more students confer about their learning. They may do so incidentally throughout the day, or a conference may be structured with a predetermined focus. Incidental peer conferences can occur whenever the student is experiencing difficulty, requires clarification or is working in collaboration with a peer. Structured conferences are usually identified at the beginning of the day, often with the teacher assigning a partner and a task. Groupings should be flexible to meet student needs.

Peer conferencing is not to be confused with peer tutoring. Peer tutoring involves work with an established set of lessons which are presented by a peer rather than a teacher; peer conferencing is more of a team effort, an equal partnership leading to learning.

Parents do not participate in peer conferencing, but teachers participate by structuring the conference. A peer conference is a great way for students to look at and monitor their own learning. As an initial step, this form of conference can lead to improved student performance, and may be used to prepare students for other forms of conferencing. Indeed, it should be done in conjunction with other forms of conferencing, not in isolation. Each type of conference serves a distinct purpose.

The peer conference allows the students to feel more comfortable, especially in admitting or recognizing their areas of difficulty. Students also tend to take suggestions better from a peer than from a teacher. Peer conferencing can go on throughout the day, without the facilitation and support of the teacher, leaving the teacher free for instruction. Much of the checking and editing of work can be done through peer conferencing, relieving teachers of some of the mechanics so that they are able to help students experiencing difficulty. However, there are some challenges. Teachers must monitor and maintain the conferences so that students remain focused on the assigned task, do not dominate one another, and find some challenge if they are doing well. Putting together students of equal ability can promote the idea of a partnership.

Student-Teacher Conference

In this type of conference, a student and a teacher discuss student strengths and areas for improvement. Students need to reflect on their own work samples, often after conferring with a peer. They would then meet with the teacher to discuss progress and future learning goals.

This form of conference has traditionally been in the classroom as a reading or writing workshop. At the secondary level, it is conducted in conjunction with an independent study project without parental participation. Process writing, as described by Donald Graves, involves students in a variety of conferences in which students examine their own writing samples, revisiting and improving their product in consultation with the teacher.

The teacher has a clear idea of what and how he or she will be assessing and evaluating, and students and teacher can work together to set goals. A student-teacher conference allows the teacher to be part of the process and to have some influence on the final product. However, students may feel uncomfortable in a one-to-one situation with the teacher and prefer a peer or group conference.

Conferencing can happen throughout the day. It can be a formal structured time when individuals or groups are scheduled in to see you. It can happen informally when you drop into a learning centre and discuss with the children what they are doing. It can even be as simple as stopping beside a child's desk and asking questions. Conferencing can also focus around entries in a learning log or a journal. It can go on when students are making other independent inquiries or are playing games. Sometimes, the presence of "learning buddies," teaching assistants, parent helpers or student teachers will enable you to focus on one particular child.

> Every child in Grade 4 was assigned a day of the cycle so that the teacher saw each child on an individual basis. This occurred during reading/writing workshop, so the other children were occupied. At the same time, a different group of children would be working each day at a peer conference centre. They had been taught to run the peer conference independently of the teacher, who only joined their conference at the end of the allotted time to discuss progress and plans.

The skills required for conferencing can be found within the existing curriculum and would have to be taught anyway. Conferencing becomes a different vehicle for teaching and showcasing such knowledge, skills and attitudes. When the class participates in reading/writing workshops, an integrated approach to the study of reading and writing, they will gain experience in peer, student-teacher, teacher-small group, and whole-class conferencing and will then find Student-Led Conferencing fairly easy to adapt to. Yes, the conferencing process requires an investment of time, but as the students learn how to conference properly, preparation time will decrease.

Parent-Teacher Conference

> In the past we came away from the parent-teacher interview feeling very disheartened. It seemed as if all of the focus was placed on my child's areas of weakness.
>
> — A Parent

The parent-teacher conference is the traditional method by which information about the student's progress is communicated to the parents. Parents receive a report and can ask questions, raise concerns, and inform teachers of any relevant information of a more personal nature that might influence the child's learning. Students are usually absent and never play an active part in the conference.

Attendance tends to be poor. Parents, particularly those for whom the language of the interview is not their first language, often find the situation uncomfortable and uninviting. There is little or no preparation for them, and as a result they have little opportunity for input into their child's learning.

HELPFUL HINTS FOR ANY PARENT-TEACHER CONFERENCE

- Sit around a table with adult-sized chairs. Don't put the desk between you and a parent.
- Relax and have a casual conversation with parents before the conference.
- Ask the parents if they would like a coffee or other beverage.
- Speak plainly — avoid the use of jargon.
- Don't intimidate parents with dress, body language or vocabulary.
- Don't write a lot during the interview; record only the pertinent points.
- Ask the parents for feedback on how they think things are going.
- Have ready more than one solution to any problem.
- Avoid surprises by anticipating possible problems.
- Provide an interpreter if needed.
- Put a Do Not Disturb sign on the door to make sure you will not be interrupted.
- If parents have more than one child in the school that will require an interview, try to make arrangements with the other teacher so that the interviews are scheduled to follow one another.
- Make sure that both you and the parents understand what has been discussed and agreed upon.
- Strive to have the interview end on a positive note.

Teachers should know that parents generally fall into one of four types: the timid, the worried, the supportive, and the critical (Larry Faas). The timid parent may be reluctant to attend a conference, address concerns and/or share information. The worried parent is concerned about student performance, and may or may not have a valid reason for feeling that way. Such a parent needs reassurance and an opportunity to talk about concerns. The supportive parent keenly wants to help and is open to suggestions pertaining to more active participation in their child's education. The critical parent will cause you the most concern. You must have evidence to support your evaluation of a child's performance and learning, especially for this type of parent. Remind such a parent that positive reinforcement and recognition of how the child has progressed along the learning continuum will benefit the child far more than focusing shortsightedly on a grade or mark.

Three-Way Conference

A Three-Way Conference involves the student, teacher and parent in a discussion centred around student achievement. As the number of team members increases, so does the time it takes to complete the conference. In this format the student takes the lead, with the direction being provided by the teacher. Students talk about their learning, teachers direct the dialogue, and parents respond, encourage and commit to a plan for future learning.

At such a conference, the participants set a growth, or action, plan, identifying future goals and assigning responsibilities to all players. Therefore, all of them must be prepared and focused on student learning. Since all members hear the same message, stressing positives and acknowledging accomplishments is important.

Student-Led Conferencing

Student-Led Conferencing calls upon the student to actively plan, implement, conduct and evaluate the parent conference, with the teacher acting as a "guide on the side." The parents are both audience members for the "performance" and thoughtful contributors.

> Minutes before the first scheduled conference, four very nervous and excited children set up their portfolios and prepare for their Student-Led Conferences. As the conferences evolve, the teacher sees parents sitting and listening attentively while students present samples of work that demonstrate their academic progress. Quiet group conversations, serious facial expressions and focused concentration are evident

among family members who have come prepared with questions to ask their children about their work, their progress and their goals. The children have been empowered to talk about their school progress.

Meanwhile, the teacher is walking around the room, monitoring and facilitating the process, not participating in the conversations unless specifically invited by a child. The teacher gathers relevant information from observing the interaction between children and parents. Parents appear to be comfortable with this format of school communication. Indeed, parents are pleased to participate in their children's learning by setting goals and helping the children achieve them. They seem a bit in awe of their children's knowledge.

There is a natural progression between the forms of conferences, leading up to Student-Led Conferences. When choosing the desired conference format, give consideration to past reporting practices, your comfort level and parents' expectations about reporting. You should **not** introduce Student-Led Conferencing without ample preparation. Letting students and parents gain experience with conferences, such as the Three-Way, may make for a smoother transition. But you can certainly launch Student-Led Conferencing without experiencing Three-Way.

> Since I had taught many of the students previously and was familiar with their parents, I chose to jump right into Student-Led Conferencing. When I first heard about Student-Led Conferencing it sounded "just right" so I was anxious to give it a try. Now I'm hooked!
>
> — A Teacher

3: On the Verge of Student-Involved Conferencing

My child was very upset, but we left him at home because we didn't believe he needed to be here (at a parent-teacher interview).

— A Parent

So, you've decided to try some form of student-involved conferencing.

First, you need to clarify for yourself the purpose, format and time requirements for a successful set of conferences. The roles people play, the nature of the agenda and the outcome will be subject to these considerations.

What type of conference will you choose? The Student-Led or the Three-Way? Each actively involves the student, but we champion Student-Led Conferencing because it places total ownership of the conference and the learning on the child.

Knowing Your Purpose

The purpose will determine the format and outcome of the conference. Is it to create a report and/or growth plan? Or, is it to discuss a report card that has already been sent home?

There should be no surprises when dealing with parents. A conference is not the time to find out that a student is experiencing difficulty. That information should be shared with parents immediately. If the conference is a forum for sharing the information that formed the basis of a report card, discussion would centre around comments and marks. But if it is the time to create a report or growth plan, then the discussion needs to focus on setting realistic, manageable goals.

Parents, teachers and students all participate in setting and monitoring the achievement of these goals.

The main purpose of the Student-Led Conference is to celebrate the student's learning and give direction for improved learning. The students meet with their parents and share their portfolios of work, discussing growth and future plans. Although the conference can generate a report card or growth plan, the main focus is to celebrate how far the student has come. As a Grade 8 student said, "This conference between the parent and the student will make everyone feel more relaxed and be able to discuss the work more easily."

The purpose of a Three-Way Conference is to share student learning and to have all three stakeholders generate a report card or growth plan for the student. The teacher retains control over the situation, with the child present to explain or clarify where necessary. The student, parent and teacher discuss and identify strengths and areas for growth. Their decisions form the basis of the report or growth plan and should be recorded, read over, agreed upon, and signed at the time so that everyone has a clear understanding of what to do to achieve success.

Format Flexibility

The age of your students does not restrict you to adoption of either the traditional parent-teacher interview or the Three-Way Conference. Not only older students can successfully lead a conference. We have seen students as young as Junior Kindergarten successfully lead conferences with their parents. All of the main components can be presented, but the actual format may vary from grade to grade. The following example with accompanying figures illustrates how you can adapt a Student-Led Conference to meet the age and maturity requirements of the students.

> During a Kindergarten Networking meeting, discussion centred around communicating with parents. When Student-Led Conferencing was mentioned, doubts were raised as to how this could be implemented with 3½ to 5 year-olds. One teacher, Mary-Lou Skinner of Denne Public School, explained how she had been involved in the early stages of implementing Student-Led Conferencing in her Junior Kindergarten classroom. The children had used a simple planner to place happy face stickers on the

centres where they felt they had accomplished the most. The teacher used a cartoon to introduce to the students the concept of Student-Led Conferencing and then led them to discuss what they would talk to their Mom and Dad about. This same planner was then the map for the Student-Led Conference for these Junior Kindergarten students and their parents, followed by a discussion between the parent and teacher regarding specific skills. Everyone contributed to the plan and they all signed it, including the student.

REFLECTIONS ON CENTRE ACTIVITIES

Name: ______________________________

JK-K CONFERENCE Date: *November 18, 1994*

Participants: *Ellen, Mr. & Mrs. McDonald, Ms. Simmons*

PERSONAL CHARACTERISTICS:
- *good imagination*
- *takes pride in her appearance*
- *leadership*
- *friendly*

SOCIAL/EMOTIONAL DEVELOPMENT:
- *determined*
- *independent*
- *confident*
- *has favourite friends*

AREAS OF INTEREST:

House Centre
Dress Up Centre
Arts and Crafts
Book Centre

LANGUAGE DEVELOPMENT:
- *speaks in complete sentences*
- *uses a clear, audible voice*
- *willing to speak in front of group*
- *does not always listen to her peers*

PHYSICAL DEVELOPMENT:
- *large & small motor skills developing at appropriate level*

READINESS SKILLS:
focus
small-muscle control — pencil grip — *good*
— use of scissors — *good*
interest in printed material — *chooses books as an activity during free time*
recognizes name, prints name, copies name *not yet*
picture-making *head and facial features*
interest in numbers/counting *yes*
matching/sorting/creating sets *up to 5*
one-to-one correspondence *yes*

Address: *43 Pleasant Ave* Telephone: *555-2121* Birthday: *March 30, 1991*

PARENT'S COMMENTS:
Cheryl is thrilled to be coming to school. I've noticed her printing letters & numbers on the chalkboard. I was very surprised to hear her talk about her work. We will practise printing her name at home.

CHILD'S COMMENTS:
(dictated) I like playing with Natalie and Kathy. I'm really good at cutting with scissors. I like to read. I want to learn to print my name by myself. I liked showing my work to Mommy and Daddy.

GOALS:
teacher — *provide tracing letters for Ellen to learn her name*
— *letter stamps to help order letters in her name*
parents — *sit with Ellen and help her to print her name*
Ellen — *will try to put her name on all her work*
— *will work with her teacher and parents to be able to print her name by next conference*

SIGNATURES: STUDENT PARENT(S) TEACHER

Ellen *Mr. & Mrs. McDonald* *Mrs. Simmons*

Time for Teachers

All student-involved conferences should be conducted at the end of a reporting period in order to set goals for the next term. Depending upon the structure of the school and timetables, conferences could take place during the day while classes are in session, on an interview day, or in the evening.

A Student-Led Conference can be scheduled during class time because the teacher is not directly participating, permitting a parent to see what is going on in the classroom. However, the conference may distract students, interfering with instruction. Space also becomes an issue and limits the number of conferences to be held. Children are less able to point out items and areas of interest or give their parents a classroom tour while lessons are being taught.

Teachers assigned to a rotary timetable face a different challenge. Is it even possible to have Student-Led Conferences when you teach four classes in the same subject area? Yes it is! With careful planning and teamwork teachers can arrange an integrated approach to conferencing.

> In one school the junior teachers developed portfolios that were appropriate for each of their grades and that would incorporate the expected learning outcomes for each subject they taught. This allowed the teachers to conduct conferences for only their homeroom classes. The teachers found that it increased their "talk" about the students and provided a more holistic picture of each student's learning.

Family dynamics may have an impact on a conference situation. When you do not have advance knowledge of parent/child dynamics, schedule a smaller number of conferences at one time. You can then be available to mediate or intervene in any conflicts that may arise.

> One parent who attended his child's conference was becoming loud and belligerent, and was disrupting conferences. When the teacher joined them, the parent continued to address his child with terms such as "stupid, lazy. . ." But the teacher was able to diffuse the parent's anger. The child was then able to continue with the conference.

Three-Way Conferences, for which the teacher is present throughout, do not pose the same problem. However, the necessity of the teacher's presence means that only one conference can take place at a time and that more overall time is required for the conferencing process.

Many school boards have set aside interview days for meeting with parents. In this instance it is possible to conduct a whole class set of Student-Led Conferences within a one-day time frame. At least four conferences can take place at one time, making such conferences a time-efficient way of communicating students' academic progress to parents. Again, Three-Way Conferences require consecutive appointments to accommodate the teacher's schedule.

So, what amount of time are we actually talking about? The average conference can take anywhere from 20 to 45 minutes. In a Student-Led Conference, you do not have to participate directly; in a Three-Way Conference, you can expect to spend 30 to 45 minutes for each child.

The student truly takes charge in a Student-Led Conference. First, there may be a 5 to 10 minute tour of the classroom and learning performances (oral reading, language game, math manipulative activity, science experiment, etc.). Students would then lead parents to the identified conference table and begin their sharing of selected work samples. It may take 5 to 15 minutes to show the samples, noticing the demonstration of strengths and the progress made over time. Then, working together, parents and students can spend 10 to 20 minutes to discuss what they heard and to set appropriate goals. You do however have the option of joining the conference for the last 5 to 10 minutes to contribute to goal setting. You can also enhance the celebration by taking an opportunity to speak to parents, if only to thank them for coming.

Whichever type of student-involved conference you decide to try first, be prepared to "sell" the idea to parents, students, and the school administration if it is unfamiliar with the practice. The next chapter should help you overcome any resistance you may encounter.

4: Venturing into Student-Led Conferencing

> What a great idea! Teach me more about Student-Led Conferencing so that I know what you need and how I can support you. There are some people that you might want to talk to . . .
>
> — Vice-Principal Margaret Roberts reacting to a teacher's interest

In this chapter, we give you the tools you will need to persuade others of the benefits of Student-Led Conferencing and indirectly, its sister, the Three-Way Conference. In so doing, we hope to strengthen your resolve to venture into this worthwhile field.

Administrative Support

Before you get into the thick of planning, be sure to inform your administrative team. Conferencing cannot occur in isolation. As with any new curriculum initiative or change in teaching practice, you will need to communicate your intentions to your school administration in order to obtain their approval and support.

Staff Education

Think about making an informal presentation to staff and colleagues about what is going to happen in your classroom. You would want to define the different types of student conferencing, focusing on Student-Led Conferencing and its purpose, benefits and the procedure involved. You are not trying to convert other teachers here. You simply want to inform staff of your intentions and plans for parent interviews, and encourage their involvement.

> Student-Led Conferencing was introduced in one of our pilot schools when a question was asked during a staff meeting. Since the teacher did not know the topic would come up, she was unprepared and felt that she wasn't able to present the concept comprehensively at that time. Nevertheless, teachers were excited by the idea and decided that they would proceed with Three-Way Conferences for their next set of interviews, not fully aware of the preparation needed. Because of that fact, the conferences did not live up to expectations. On reflection, the teachers realized that they needed to better prepare themselves, the students, and their parent community for conferencing. Their eagerness to continue with conferencing and their need for support led them to initiate a network with their peers.

An informal presentation on Student-Led Conferencing might follow this agenda:

SAMPLE AGENDA FOR STAFF MEETING

1. Relationship between school reporting procedures and communicating student achievement
2. Definition of the types of conferencing:
   - Peer
   - Parent-Teacher
   - Parent-Teacher-Student (Three-Way)
   - Student-Led
3. Connection with portfolios
4. Benefits of forms of conferences:
   - To student
   - To parent
   - To teacher
5. Implications of conferencing for classroom program
6. Question and answer period

School-Wide Adoption

If an entire school adopts student-involved conferencing, you and your colleagues will have to determine several things. What format will be used? Will the entire school use this format? Only one division? One grade level? Only your own class? Determining the time frame for the conference is also important: consider how often and when your school reports student progress to parents.

Develop your timeline for implementation based on your comfort level, past experience, current school practices, the students and what you know of the community. You will probably need to introduce the process of Student-Led Conferencing slowly and in stages to allow for success. A natural transition is from the traditional parent-teacher conference to the Three-Way Conference, where the student participates too, for a few times. Then once you have gained some expertise and the students are familiar with the conferencing process and the skills involved, you can move on to Student-Led Conferences, which the students will now be better equipped to conduct.

Parent Orientation Meeting

Plan a parent orientation meeting to enable parents to understand the process of conferencing. We recommend that, once you check to see that your proposed date does not conflict with other school activities, you send a personal invitation to the evening early in the school year to initiate the process. (See the sample.) What do you do if parents are unable to attend? Do you offer an additional meeting, send a letter home or make personal phone calls? Chances are that no one method will do to reach all parents. You will have to try many ways in order to ensure parental knowledge, understanding and support for the process. And don't forget to invite your school's principal or vice-principal. Their presence indicates support for the chosen conference format.

At this meeting, you can provide parents with an overview of the curriculum. In order for them to have realistic expectations for their child, they need to get familiar with the widely held expectations for that grade. *Supporting Learning*, a British Columbia government document, calls these "frames of reference that help parents and teachers focus on the development of the individual child." You can provide parents with **exemplars**, samples of appropriate texts that will encompass the range of acceptable performances for the appropriate grade level. "I would like to know more about all of the subjects that you study, judged in this manner. This would help me in charting your regular progress on a day-to-day basis," said a parent later.

Dear Parents,

I have been asked to participate in a project called "Student-Led Conferencing." It is a part of the Outcome Based Learning thrust that the York Region Board of Education is promoting as a more effective way for our students to learn. Three teachers across the region are taking part in the project to provide feedback as to how successful this is for students, parents and teachers. Our class has been asked to participate as the intermediate class.

This is a somewhat different approach to parent interviews and so I am starting this very slowly and carefully. I have chosen six students at random to take part in student-led conferencing for the first term. During the second term I hope to be able to increase the number to half the class (fifteen students) and in the last term I would like to try this with the whole class.

Interviews are available for any of the students in our class on the evening of December 1st or during the day on December 2nd. The six initial students and their parents are asked to meet on the evening of November 30th. Following the six student-led conferences if these parents wish a private interview to discuss specific matters this would be arranged.

For the student-led conferences the students will receive their parents in the classroom in order to show their work and discuss their progress. In preparation for these interviews the students are learning to accept responsibility and be accountable for their own work and behaviour. They have been involved in recognising their individual strong points and in deciding which areas they would most like to improve on next term.

I hope that this letter has clearly explained the changes in the parent interview session for the first term with our class. Please call me at the school if you have any questions or if anything is unclear.

Yours truly,

Mrs. S.A. Landy

Name of student ______________________________

My child is taking part in the student-led conferences. I am available for an interview on Wednesday November 30th at 7.30 or 8.00 p.m. (Please circle the convenient time.)

I would like an interview on Thursday December 1st/Friday December 2nd. (Please circle the convenient date.)

Please choose an appropriate time. Thurs Dec. 1st 6.00-9.00 p.m. or Friday Dec 2nd. 9.00-4.00 ____________________

Outline the different forms of conferencing and explain how a Student-Led Conference differs from the traditional parent-teacher interview. In doing so you can effectively provide parents with a rationale for this new way of reporting students' learning, while providing an outline of the process of Student-Led Conferencing.

The following summary may assist you in developing your personal rationale.

> In answer to increasing concerns about accountability and improved student learning, educators are trying to identify more appropriate methods of communicating student progress. One of the methods to achieve all this is Student-Led Conferencing which directly involves the students. Since the discussion centres on the students and their learning, they must be present. After all, they should be able to discuss their learning and identify future directions. The responsibility for a child's academic progress lies squarely on the child's shoulders in Student-Led Conferencing. This process develops the body of knowledge, skills and attitudes that we believe students will require for the future and addresses current concerns.

You may want to provide articles or discuss current research on how children learn to make the connection between research and classroom practice easier for parents to understand. This research will identify contributions to student learning as well as the benefits of such conferencing and the development of skills that students will require in the future. You can draw on articles referred to in the bibliography of this book.

Tell parents about the many benefits of Student-Led Conferencing for them. These, as well as the benefits for students and the teacher, are outlined in "What Are the Benefits of Student-Led Conferencing?"

Here is some testimony:

> When Jennifer was little I was always involved, and I felt that I was losing that now that she is getting older. Student-Led Conferencing is giving it back to me.
>
> — A Parent

It allows us to truly spend the time listening to her and to be appreciative of her efforts.

— A Parent

Highlight all the benefits of Student-Led Conferencing to help parents understand why you are implementing this type of conferencing.

If possible, offer parents a sample session of a Student-Led Conference, through a role play between teachers or a videotape. This would provide them with a clearer picture of what to expect. Once they understand what the conference will look like, they will be able to visualize how several conferences could take place simultaneously. They will see that even though several are going on at the same time, everyone will be so involved in their own conversations that they won't pay any attention to what is going on around them. They will have privacy.

Clearly identify expectations to encourage maximum support and contributions by parents, perhaps referring to "How Parents Can Support Their Children," on page 44-45. One pilot teacher found that providing parents with specific, guiding questions to help prepare them to participate in a meaningful dialogue about student work and progress was particularly useful. Having parents clearly aware of what is expected of them will contribute to the overall success of the conference.

At the orientation meeting, explain to parents what a portfolio is and how it can be used to report student progress. You might show a sample portfolio so that parents can become familiar with it. The role of portfolios will be discussed in detail in Chapter 7.

Encourage parents to recognize that their child's portfolio will provide evidence of student growth along the learning continuum. The communication of student progress will allow parents to form a more realistic expectation of student achievement. Parents need a frame of reference within which to examine their own expectations for their child's learning. For example, parents may believe that their child is reading quite well when the child is reading primary text. On attending the orientation meeting and examining the reading material that the rest of the students are able to read, they will realize that their child is experiencing difficulty. Similarly, some children can do mathematical computations perfectly and not understand the meaning of the operations involved. Again, you can make

WHAT ARE THE BENEFITS OF STUDENT-LED CONFERENCING?

For the Students . . .
- accountability for their learning
- ownership for progress in learning
- increased commitment to school work because they present to parents
- increased interaction between child and parents
- independence
- self-assessment
- active participation in the evaluation process
- learning of real-life skills
- increased self-confidence
- enhanced self-esteem
- development of leadership skills
- empowerment
- fostering of organizational, communication, and critical thinking skills

For the Parents . . .
- assumption of a significant role to play in their child's learning
- active participation in their child's learning
- better understanding of that learning
- less intimidating environment
- first-language communication
- forum for parents to have a voice
- more relaxed atmosphere
- better communication between home and school
- a forum for parents to talk to their child productively and positively

For the Teacher . . .
- increased student participation
- increased parental involvement
- more effective use of interview time
- after the initial stage, less work!
- gain of partners to help write the repord card/growth plan
- freedom to take on an observing role

parents aware of the distinction between being able to do computations and being able to understand the process.

Let parents know that their children will introduce growth plans, which they have drafted with your help, at the Student-Led Conferences for the parents' input and clarification. Parents need to appreciate their role in developing and implementing the plans. They play a significant part in identifying strengths, goals and responsibilities related to their children's learning process. You might want to show a sample growth plan to parents at the orientation meeting.

Time should be left at the end of the evening for you to address questions or concerns that parents may have. Parents may question the validity of this new conference approach, as well as the students' ability to be responsible for and to conduct the conference. An outline of some common concerns and responses that you can use as reference or as a handout to parents appears on pages 41-42.

You may want to provide a handout outlining the key points of the orientation session and/or a brief summary of the conference. Doing so is especially helpful if one parent is absent. The other parent can then use it as a way of sharing the information.

> I think the concept is great. It gives students an understanding of where they need to work harder and to really be proud of presenting their work to parents.
>
> — A Parent

Approaches to Students

You will have to introduce your students to the concept of "conferencing." You will probably want to do this by talking about conferencing in general, and then Student-Led Conferencing, in particular. To make it more meaningful to students, first discuss conference forms they are already familiar with: conferencing with peers for speeches, practising for a play, conferencing with the teacher, and conferencing about process writing and rough drafts of projects.

Talk about how the students participating in Student-Led Conferencing will benefit. Just as all learning must be relevant, students need to know the purpose behind such conferencing. You can review the benefits to students that appear in "What Are the Benefits of Student-Led Conferencing?" earlier in the chapter. Students might translate these benefits as on page 42.

SOME PARENT CONCERNS AND TEACHER RESPONSES

- ***I think it is your job as the teacher to conduct the conference. You're the one with the expertise.***
  - — The students know about their learning better than anybody else and will have been taught what standards they are striving to meet.
  - — Students are taught the skills to self-reflect, self-assess, set goals, and monitor their learning.
  - — The students have the most at stake.
  - — I will clearly set expectations and roles for all players prior to the conference to eliminate the expertise problem.
- ***How can my child, who is only in Kindergarten, conduct a conference?***
  - — The breadth and depth of the conference will vary from grade to grade.
  - — Students are taught to do what is appropriate for their age and grade.
  - — Students will discuss the same issues, but not in the same detail as older students.
- ***I'm not able to attend the scheduled Student-Led Conference. I work nights and sleep during the day. I have no time.***
  - — You can invite another adult, such as a member of the staff, principal, or guidance counsellor.
  - — The conference can be held at home.
- ***I would like to have a private interview without my child.***
  - — I am happy to meet with you privately in addition to your participating in a Student-Led Conference.
- ***My son and I always argue whenever we talk about his school work.***
  - — If a disagreement occurs a teacher then joins the group and redirects the discussion.
- ***Can I bring the baby with me?***
  - — I strongly discourage this.
  - — Please plan in advance for this event.
  - — The school will strive to provide babysitting service.
- ***What happens to the portfolios at the end of the year?***
  - — Sometimes the district/board makes the decision.
  - — Portfolios can be sent home or passed on to the next teacher.
  - — With students' permission, some can be kept and shared as exemplars.

- ***I expect my child to get straight As.***
  - — I can provide you with grade-level expectations.
  - — Learning is a continuum. It's developmental.
  - — I can show you exemplars of work and appropriate text samples — we don't necessarily use grade marks.
- ***How can I help my child to set and achieve realistic goals?***
  - — I will keep you informed about what is going on in the classroom, beginning with the parent information night.
  - — We will break down learning outcomes into "bits" which can be more easily achieved.
  - — Plan to identify the steps involved in reaching goals.
- ***How can my child advise me on how I can help him?***
  - — Suggestions have been generated through an earlier student-teacher conference.
  - — You will receive guidelines or suggestions as to how you can support your child's learning.
  - — Children know what they need, and working together with you, their parents, they can identify ways for you to help.

- I can show off to my parents, brag about my learning — be successful!
- I get to be in charge and direct my own learning.
- I can feel good about what I can do and what I have achieved.
- I can learn to communicate more effectively.
- I can get help with things I need help with.

You'll also have to tell students what is expected of them. For example, they will have to select learning outcomes (goals), develop the process that they will use to achieve the learning, select work samples, determine how they will evaluate the product and reflect on the learning. Reassure students that they will learn how to handle all stages of the conference through classroom activities.

Both students and parents may initially feel daunted by all that they have to do for a Student-Led Conference so encourage them throughout the process. They are bound to find it worthwhile. "I never believed I could talk to my parents like that about my school work," said one Grade 8 student. "I could answer every question they asked." Student-Led Conferences are all about responsibility and the confident ownership of learning.

5: Roles and Responsibilities

> Mom, I'm in charge of the interview. If you have any questions, just ask me.
>
> — An ESL Student

Parents, students and teachers all contribute much to the success of Student-Led Conferences. Clearly understanding their respective roles and responsibilities can make a big difference to the outcome.

The Parents

You must rely on the parents to accept their children's invitation to the conference and to remember to attend. Parents should respond not just out of courtesy but also to ensure that their child has an adult present at conference time. Doing this shows a commitment to the child.

However, you might wonder if all parents will receive their invitations. The higher the grade, the more likely it is that the notes and messages will not get home. Students may worry about what their parents will hear during a traditional interview and avoid letting their parents know about the interview nights. They realize that negative aspects may be highlighted more than positive ones during the interview. Also, they often don't see the relevance of the interview. Once students become involved in conferencing, however, their fears are alleviated. They become part of the conference, contributing to the direction and content under discussion.

You might also wonder if you'll encounter balky parents. Many teachers have experienced the lack of parental attendance at school events, such as curriculum nights or open house evenings. Usually, these events do not include direct performances by the students. Our three very different pilot schools confirmed that attendance miraculously improves when students "perform."

When the conference is really important to the children, they will make sure that their parents attend. "He would give us no peace until we came. We had to cancel another appointment in order to be here," said one parent. At the same time, as parents become involved with the school and the child through conferencing, that participation demonstrates to the child a commitment to the child's learning.

Once at the conference, ideal parents will listen actively, and support and encourage their child. We cannot assume that parents understand what all that means, however. We recommend that you explain such terms as "active listening" and provide examples relevant to a conference. You could do this during the parent orientation meeting or by handing out "How Parents Can Support Their Children."

HOW PARENTS CAN SUPPORT THEIR CHILDREN

"The three of them sat at the table. As the child spoke, the parents leaned forward and appeared intent on the words spoken. At intervals they encouraged their child with smiles and praise, while clarifying what they heard with questions and comments."

Active Listening
Active listening requires focused attention on your child and what is being said. You need to know what you are listening for and should be able to retell what you've heard. Asking questions for clarification is part of active listening.

Supporting and Encouraging
You can provide your child with support in several ways. By making positive comments and asking pertinent questions at appropriate intervals you will provide your child with the confidence he/she needs to continue. Encouraging smiles, positive body language and ongoing indications of interest all help to create a comfortable atmosphere.

Sample Questions or Comments for Parents to Use during the Conference

- **Make positive comments.**
  "I'm really proud of the work that you have shown us."
  "I can see that you are getting better at . . ."
  "I can see that you tried very hard."
  "I'm so impressed with the way you conducted your conference."
- **Ask specific questions about your child's work/learning.**
  "Why did you choose to share this particular piece of work?"
  "What learning does this work show?"
  "What will you learn next?"
- **Give positive feedback.**
  "I can really see the growth in your . . ."
  "I'm amazed that you know how to . . ."
  "I didn't know you could . . ."
- **Express confidence in your child's ability to lead the conference.**
  "I can see that you are really organized and ready to begin your conference."
  "You are doing a great job conducting this conference."
  "I can hardly wait until your next conference."
  "I know that you are very talented. Today I have seen many examples of your talents."
- **Help your child to formulate goals.**
  "Now that we have seen your work, what do you think you should work on next?"
  "What steps will you need to follow to reach your goal?"
  "Are these goals possible? Is your timeline reasonable?"
  "What can I do to help you reach your goals?"
  "How will you know when you have reached your goal?"

As part of the learning team, parents contribute significantly to the goal setting required for the development of their child's growth plan. They depend upon the teacher to introduce the concept to facilitate their contribution to the completion of the plan at the end of the conference.

Sometimes parents have unrealistic expectations and feel their child is not performing according to widely held expectations. That's because they have no basis for comparison, a problem that is especially true for a first or only child. If the teacher shares work samples at the parent orientation meeting that reflect this continuum, the parents can understand how students develop during the course of the year. They need to remember that the conference should focus on student strengths and accomplishments.

Parents need to understand that time is an important ingredient in learning anything. They need to remember that each child is unique and that rates of development vary. For example, not all children learn to talk or walk at the same time. "All students can learn, but not at the same time, in the same way, or on the same day," affirmed William Spady, the leader of the outcome-based education movement. However, if a child does not progress by a certain set stage, it would raise concern and require intervention. Parents must show patience.

At the conclusion of the conference, ask parents to reflect on the process and product of the conference, and to record their compliments and comments in the guest book provided. They should also write a brief post-conference reflection letter to their child and send it to the school within the following week. This action validates student learning and ownership in the reporting process, motivating students and contributing to their self-confidence.

Dear Bryan,

We were very happy to attend your presentation on Friday. We noticed you sat down and got ready to present right away. You had your folder organized and you took charge. We were very proud of you and your efforts. The work you chose to show to us were pages that you had done well on and it was so nice to see how proud you were of it.

We do agree with Ms. Walford, we would also like to see you improve on your note taking, your neatness of your written work and the flow of sentences.

Bryan, your confidence is really blooming. You showed us how well you could speak out and share your thoughts. It is a real gift being able to talk out in front of a group and you'll find it to be a lifetime skill. You are gaining some important skills. Your math is becoming solid, as well as your French. We are so pleased to see you enjoy reading as much as you are.

We know you have difficulty expressing your thoughts and writing them on paper, but keep on working hard and it will come along also. You should have noticed how some things you once struggled with are now starting to come to you a little easier.

Being active and participating will gain you so much experience that you can use for the rest of your life. We know that you put forth an extra effort in improving your grades and trying to be more organized.

We would like to help you out as much as we can. You know we will always be there for you whenever problems arise or even if you just want to talk to us.

We love you very much. You have made us so proud. Keep up the hard work and enjoy what you're doing.

Love Mom
& Dad

The Students

In order to have a successful conference, students must prepare themselves for their active role. They are responsible for selecting work samples for their portfolios and articulating the reasons for their choices based upon a list of stated criteria. These criteria are established in advance by the classroom teacher or by the teacher and students working together. (See Chapter 7 for more information about choosing work samples.)

After they have learned conferencing skills, students will need to role-play and rehearse with a variety of audiences. Doing this increases self-confidence and may relieve some of their anxiety about the conference. "Everytime I practised, I got better," said a Grade 3 student.

Students can help make parents feel welcome by designing and creating a personal invitation to attend their Student-Led Conference. They could mail this invitation home or hand deliver it about two weeks prior to the conference. The invitation, which parents should be expecting, should include the date, time and location of the conference, as well as a brief description and an R.S.V.P. If they wish, they could use a letter such as the one on the next page.

Students may also be able to make parents feel welcome by greeting them at the classroom door, introducing them to their teacher, and providing a guided tour of their classroom. After that, they can provide parents with the materials required for the conference, and actually conduct it. Both students and parents should fill in reflection guides and address the development of a growth plan at this time. Students should later write a thank-you note to their parents or guests for attending their conference.

Date: ____________

Dear __________:

I am happy to invite you to attend my portfolio conference on _________. It will be held in room _____ at _____ a.m./p.m. I will be sharing this term's work with you and hope you will help me set my goals for next term.

Please R.S.V.P. by __________________ so that my teacher can schedule our conference.

LOVE,

____

- -

_____ Yes, I'd love to attend your conference.
_____ No, I'm sorry I cannot attend as scheduled. A better time/or day for me would be _________________.
_____ I am unable to attend the conference.

Parent/guardian signature ______________________

Dear Mom and Dad:

Thank you for coming to my conference and looking at my work. I wanted to show you that I have done really well on my hundreds and reading. I was glad when you said that you are really proud of my reading. I'm glad you are going to help me with my spelling at home. Now I know my spelling will get better.

Love,
Steven

The Teacher

As we've already mentioned, the first step in initiating any new program in the school is to inform your administrative team. Doing so is both a courtesy and a critical component of the success of the conferences. You want the main office to be able to deal with parent inquiries effectively and knowledgeably. No one likes to be left in the dark. Early in the school year, publish a newsletter article for the school community explaining and outlining the implementation of Student-Led Conferencing. This will alert parents that something new is going to take place.

Once you have the green light from administration, take time to set out the process and timeline involved in Student-Led Conferencing through the development of long-range plans. (See "Organizational Calendar" for sample long-range plans.) These plans should take into account the needs of your students, their parents and the school community. Expect to plan responsively, revisiting what you've drafted as you progress through the identified steps.

An organizational calendar that reflects the lessons you will need to teach and the conference-related activities you will need to coordinate follows. Subsequent chapters outline these more fully.

Closer to the time of the conferences, you will need to create a master list and schedule calendar. Be sensitive to those children whose parents/guardians cannot attend. Where appropriate, help arrange for alternative adults to participate in the conference — every child must have an adult present at the conference. If you learn that grandparents, aunts and uncles, godparents or older siblings are unavailable, try to enlist the principal, another teacher, a librarian or a resource teacher on the student's behalf.

As noted earlier, in a Student-Led Conference you take on the role of an observer. Enter the parent-student dialogue only when invited to or when necessary to change the direction of the interview. You may also choose to join the conference during the last ten minutes of goal setting. Observing is one of the most rewarding roles for the teacher. It allows you to watch the family dynamics, gaining valuable insight into how your students listen and talk, what is significant to them and how confident they are. This in turn increases the effectiveness of instruction.

Although the goal of Student-Led Conferencing is to increase the ownership of the students of their own learning and to enable them to lead conferences, without careful preparation and facilitation by the teacher none of that will come to fruition.

ORGANIZATIONAL CALENDAR - FIRST MONTH

	Monday	*Tuesday*	*Wednesday*	*Thursday*	*Friday*
Week 1		• discuss plans with admin.			• gather materials for portfolios
Week 2	• introduce "conferencing"	• introduce "portfolio" and choose type • personalize and store	• introduce "reflection" • model process of "self-reflection"	• discuss "peer evaluation"	• "exemplars" • "rubrics"
Week 3	• parent guide to be available on parent orientation night		• time management • organization		
Week 4		• letter writing lesson "invitations to parent night"	• invitations go home • parent reflection sheet sent home		

ORGANIZATIONAL CALENDAR - SECOND MONTH

	Monday	*Tuesday*	*Wednesday*	*Thursday*	*Friday*
Week 1			• parent orientation mtg.		
Week 2	• verbal skills	• listening skills		• design/make guest book for parents	
Week 3	• work sample selection	• individual student conferences for choosing pieces begin			
Week 4	• growth/action plans				

ORGANIZATIONAL CALENDAR – THIRD MONTH

	Monday	*Tuesday*	*Wednesday*	*Thursday*	*Friday*
Week 1		• model conference • role play			• parent note re time/ date for conference
Week 2		• social skills – introductions – politeness – dress		• conflict management (role play)	• master copy of schedule • begin to find other adults for students who need them
Week 3			• ask librarian about using library	• discuss refreshments	• send letter to parents re ingredients
Week 4		• decorations and signs			• agendas completed • work samples selected

ORGANIZATIONAL CALENDAR – FOURTH MONTH

	Monday	*Tuesday*	*Wednesday*	*Thursday*	*Friday*
Week 1	• baking/storing refreshments • send reminder home re Friday's conferences				☆ Conference Day • see list
Week 2	• thank-you notes to parents • debriefing of students	• student reflection • teacher shares reflection			• Celebration! • parent reflections distributed to students • treats
Week 3	• BEGIN AGAIN! (include revisions and modifications to process and lessons)				
Week 4					

6: Teaching Students Necessary Skills

I was really worried that I had not prepared the children adequately, that the conference might only last two minutes and that the rest would be silence. My fears proved to be groundless.

— A Teacher

Start early in the school year to teach students the specific skills they need for successful conferencing: skills that will contribute to their overall performance and that will enhance lifelong learning. These skills include self-reflection, self-assessment, communication, decision making, problem solving, time management, organization and conflict management. Chapters such as **Reflecting on Learning** and **Portfolios** discuss some of these in more detail.

You might want to develop an organizational calendar, such as the one at the end of the previous chapter, to show which skills need to be developed and when. Of course, student needs and class progress will temper this, and you will still want to allow for spontaneous "teachable moments."

Plan to teach the necessary skills separately as specific class lessons and then to incorporate them into the regular classroom instruction to teach in the content areas. In your zeal to promote them, though, be sure not to overlook subject-specific skills such as mapping and multiplication of fractions. Subject-specific skills should be addressed because curriculum still dictates content knowledge.

Sequential Lessons

The following chart provides a set of lessons common to all grade levels. The amount of time required and the degree of structure for a lesson will depend upon the grade level and maturity of your students. For example, a Kindergarten class may simply sign a thank-you note written by the teacher, a Grade 2 student may copy a thank-you note from chart paper, and a Grade 8 student will be able to write a thank-you note independently.

The lesson numbers indicate the sequential order, **not** the number of lessons. Each lesson may be taught over several days, or even weeks. It may take several "visits" before students show that they have internalized the material and can do it.

SEQUENTIAL STEPS FOR PREPARING STUDENTS
FOR STUDENT-LED CONFERENCING

Lesson One
- introduction of the various types of conferencing
- rationale for conferencing (relevancy)
- benefits

Lesson Two
- portfolios: introduction of the concept
- discussion of types
- expectations re: portfolio and its use
- management issues

Lesson Three
- making the portfolio
- determining portfolio storage and access
- getting the portfolios physically organized

Lesson Four
- self-evaluation, reflection — value to student
- exemplars — expectations
- How do I learn best?
- honest reflection

Lesson Five
- evaluation — self, peer, teacher
- value of peer evaluation
- types of peer evaluation — partner, group, whole class

Lesson Six
- social skills/behavior — introductions, politeness, respect, active listening
- dress — appropriate for occasion, cultural group and socio-economic conditions

Lesson Seven
- communication: *writing skills* — invitations; thank-you notes; letters.

Lesson Eight
- communication: *verbal skills* — effective articulation of ideas and feelings; tone of voice; eye contact; exchange of ideas.

Lesson Nine
- communication: *listening skills* — active listening; courtesy; taking turns.

Lesson Ten
- time management — scheduling work time effectively; personal time accountability.

Lesson Eleven
- work sample selection — students choosing pieces of work that best demonstrate their abilities "to date"; based on shared criteria.

Lesson Twelve
- organizational skills — getting ready for the conference; setting a student agenda for the conference; keeping to a timetable.

Lesson Thirteen
- conflict management — role play of different types of conflict which may arise during a conference; discussion of possible solutions to problems.

Lesson Fourteen
- subject-specific skills — clarification of subject skills so that students can explain them to their parents; review of work samples that demonstrate their levels of accomplishment, e.g., an exercise showing the math skill of multiplication.

The Need to Teach Self-Assessment

Take care to identify appropriate learning outcomes, or goals, based on the developmental level of the child. These may differ from grade level expectations. Attainable goals will lead to continued success. The process that students will use to learn relates directly to their own personal learning styles. "A person's learning style is the [multiple] intelligences put to work," wrote Robert Marzano. Even though students have a preferred style, encourage them to choose not only those activities which reflect that learning style but also those which will help develop other learning styles. Choice plays a vital role in the motivation and commitment of the student and contributes to the overall quality of the product.

ASSESSMENT FRAMEWORK FOR MEASURING STUDENT PERFORMANCE

Strand: *Writing* Grade: *4*

Learning Outcome: *Purpose — Adapts and uses language for a variety of purposes in different contexts through various media*

Performance Criteria: *writes fiction and non-fiction*

Performance demonstrated	*Assessment rating*
• *gathers info. from several sources* • *uses an original planner* • *info. presented in a creative way* • *paraphrases*	4 Demonstrating performance beyond expectations for grade
• *makes point-form notes* • *uses planner to organize information* • *writes expository text using info. from point-form notes* • *paraphrases*	3 Consistent demonstration of mastery at grade level
• *beginning to make pt. form notes* • *copies text* • *needs help to organize info. on planner*	2 Not yet consistent demonstration of mastery
• *not able to write pt. form notes* • *not ready to use planner* • *copies text without understanding of text*	1 Beginning to work toward mastery

Students will need to be taught how to select the pieces of work that best reflect what they have learned. In order to do this effectively, they require exemplars, or student samples that set the standard so that students can clearly see what is expected. "What does an 'A' look like?" The expectations should be clear and attainable and the criteria should be shared with the students before the work has even begun. Students need to know exactly what is acceptable and what is not. They will need to be able to evaluate their own work and that of their peers. In order to do this successfully, they will have to know what the product should look like.

One way that students can evaluate their work is to use a scoring guide that may be shared with them by the teacher before they begin or developed in class. Such guides, or **rubrics**, provide a rating scale of the criteria levels leading to an assessment rating, mark, level or grade. "Assessment Framework for Measuring Student Performance" is a sample rubric prepared by a teacher. It clearly describes what is expected of students and can promote purposeful reflection. As workshop leader Richard Stiggins said in May 1993, "If you wish to maximize learning, teach students to assess themselves."

Rehearsing the Conference

Plan to model the conference itself, including introduction skills and reflection practices. You may even choose to show a video of a previous conference so that students can see what the conference looks and sounds like. Or, you could model parent behavior with a student volunteer for the whole class and ask for feedback.

One way to initiate role-play conversations in the classroom is to have students respond to an open-ended sentence, for example:

- One thing I learned today was . . .
- One question I thought of today was . . .
- One thing I found very hard today was . . .
- Something I never did before was . . .
- I'm still wondering about . . .
- Tomorrow, I want to find the answer to . . .

Provide many opportunities for students to practise what they have seen — as with any performance, they need much rehearsal. Older students, such as learning buddies or peer tutors, can help students prepare for the final conference. They can take the parental role and also provide feedback.

> One Grade 8 teacher uses her teacher's aide to act as a parent to provide rehearsal for the conference. The resource teacher also comes in as an observer to provide feedback to students following the role-play scenarios.

But even without such help, students can enact conferences with some students taking parental roles. These rehearsals enable students to get reaction and advice in a non-threatening environment.

Have students complete self-reflections after each practice. They might consider the questions below.

- What was most satisfying and why?
- What, if anything, proved to be difficult?
- What plan do I have for improvement?
- Do I have clear steps to follow?
- What progress have I made on my growth plan?

You can also hold daily debriefings after the mock conferences. Remember to let students brainstorm "worse-case scenarios," such as a parent yelling, not listening or refusing to let the student lead the conference, and to come up with possible solutions.

> Practice is the most important thing.
>
> — A Teacher

7: Portfolios

> The original analogy for portfolio assessment was the artist's portfolio. Artists carry their completed, polished works in a portfolio that they show to prospective clients. In effect, artists use a portfolio to show what they can do, how versatile and how good their work can be.
>
> — Robert Marzano, *Assessing Student Outcomes*

Merriam-Webster's definition of a portfolio is "a hinged cover or flexible case for carrying loose papers, pictures or pamphlets." As classroom teachers, we consider a portfolio to be a collection of student work reflecting learning progress. Both process and product need to be documented. The portfolio provides a vehicle for reflecting on and considering a child's ability. The sharing of the portfolio is an example of authentic assessment.

A Reflection of the Whole Child

The portfolio clearly lays out the child's learning for all partners in the assessment process to reflect on the child's growth over time. It documents significant student outcomes and provides evidence of learning for student, teacher, parents and the community. For parents, the portfolio represents the child's growth; for students, the portfolio is a celebration of their accomplishments.

At its best, a portfolio reflects the whole child. It is positive in focus, not negative, and is filled with the "I can do . . ." of the child. It provides a picture of what students know and can do, and is full of "snapshots" of student learning at specific times during the year. The collection of samples, chosen with or without student input, should be an ongoing part of the classroom experience. As a tracking mechanism, the portfolio then forms the basis of reporting to parents, showing growth towards mastery. The greater the variety of work samples, the more complete the picture of the child.

The use of the portfolio in conferencing permits ongoing reflection on the teaching-learning process. There is discussion on setting goals and on growth plans for mastering new knowledge, skills and attitudes. Conferencing around a portfolio may take place between students; teacher and student; teacher and parent; parent, teacher and student; or parent and student. There are many individuals with whom the child could conference, but the most significant are the parents.

The key aspect of portfolio use is the discussion and self-reflection that surrounds the work samples in the portfolio, supporting and enhancing cognitive development. Students consider questions such as "How do I learn?" "When do I learn best?" "What do I find difficult?" "Why is this my best piece?" "What learning does this (sample) show?" In order to use the portfolio effectively, complex thinking must be brought to bear upon it; this will result in valuable insight into student learning.

Thomas Armstrong, in *Multiple Intelligences in the Classroom*, identifies five uses for portfolios:

1. *Celebration:* To acknowledge and validate students' products and accomplishments during the year
2. *Cognition:* To help students reflect upon their own work
3. *Communication:* To let parents, administrators and other teachers know about students' learning progress
4. *Cooperation:* To provide a means for groups of students to collectively produce and evaluate their own work
5. *Competency:* To establish criteria by which a student's work can be compared to that of other students or to a standard or benchmark

Choosing the Right Format

There is no single format for a portfolio. In some cases, your board of education will predetermine it so you won't have to make a decision. The format chosen will vary from student to student, teacher to teacher, class to class, year to year. Portfolios could be anything from photo albums with adhesive pages to boxes to student-constructed ones. Each type has its own advantages and disadvantages which are noted below. Remember that the purpose of the portfolio is to track and monitor evidence of student learning.

WHAT FORMS CAN THE PORTFOLIO TAKE?

Form	*Advantages*	*Disadvantages*
photo album	samples easily added or removed pages clean and neat due to plastic covering	sample size limited flat samples only no tapes storage demands
scrapbooks	variety in size and samples easily stored	samples glued permanently no tapes less durable
accordion files	expandable access to samples audio tapes possible novelty factor	sample size limited no video tapes storage demands
hanging files	sturdy expandable audio tapes possible but tight fit easily stored	sample size limited no video tapes
commercial	no flexibility no personalization attractive format clear to follow	sample size limited no tapes storage depends upon size
binders	easy to add, delete what you want continuous	sample size limited storage demands no tapes
boxes	flexible sizes "in/out" access tapes possible	storage demands access to boxes
student-made	personal suited to purpose	messy

Two items that you can make great use of, regardless of the type of portfolio chosen, are a camera and a date stamp.

If we are tracking student progress, dates on work become essential. Students are quite capable of date-stamping and organizing their work; teachers should not have to do that for them.

You can use a camera to capture learning episodes that otherwise could not be shown or reflected by paper and pencil; for example, participation in a concert or the building of a three-dimensional structure. Polaroid cameras have the advantage of providing instant evidence; however, the cost of film may deter you from them. Regular cameras have the advantage of allowing multiple prints to be made at a reduced cost. You can thereby show parents and others work products that cannot be taken home, for example, bulletin board displays. The pictures themselves allow parents to join in the classroom experience and see students learning.

If your budget permits, a video camera can be an invaluable resource. Students can record special classroom events, capture evidence of active learning, and take the classroom home.

Also, regardless of type, encourage students to personalize their portfolios, perhaps adding a photograph or self-portrait, illustrations they consider meaningful, logos or designs, written-out anecdotes, or images of famous people or heroes.

The type of portfolio you choose will depend on practical considerations, such as sample size, storage availability, and the need for durability; portfolio purpose, for example, tracking skills only or conferencing; lifespan — one grade or for a division; and focus — whether the portfolio is subject specific, contains integrated subjects, or reflects the whole child.

"Storage Considerations for Portfolios" outlines the advantages and disadvantages of various storage options. The section that follows discusses more practical issues.

- *Sample size*

When selecting portfolio size, keep in mind that a portfolio serves as a way to collect learning evidence. Primary children who are developing fine-motor skills need to have larger portfolios to accommodate larger sized work products. Their work should not be folded. If you have ever taught a primary class, you'll know that young children love glue and use so much of it that you often can't unfold glued work samples. Other students can work within a smaller format; however, collection of work samples should not be limited to 8½ × 11 inch paper. The grade level of your students may well affect sample size.

STORAGE CONSIDERATIONS FOR PORTFOLIOS

Type	*Advantages*	*Disadvantages*
inverted desks/ sawhorses	cheap, very large samples held, easily accessible by students	floor space demands, possibly messy
file cabinets	durable, accessible, a novelty for students, part of the classroom furniture	sample size limited, no video tapes, not mobile, cost
banker's boxes	cheap, mobile, different sizes, hanging files option, easily accessible, durable and stackable	sample size limited, storage demands
plastic storage bins/chests	durable, different sizes, hanging files accommodated in some, storage for video and audio tapes	storage demands
wheeled (tiered) carts	durable, mobile, easy access	sample size limited
magazine boxes	different sizes, durable, mobile, audio and video tapes held	storage, sample size limited, less structured
record holders/pot lid holders	any size portfolio, readily accessible by students, durable, cheap	messy

Sometimes the portfolio size is determined by whether or not the portfolio is subject specific. For example, an art portfolio must be much larger than a writing portfolio. A student portfolio may also need to accommodate audio and video tapes and other larger work samples, particularly if it will be used to reflect the whole child. Being able to see and hear the child provides evidence that cannot be captured by pencil-and-paper tasks. For example, a child whose talent lies in gymnastics has traditionally not been able to share accomplishments with parents. A video tape would allow the sharing of such a performance.

SOME WAYS OF STORING PORTFOLIOS

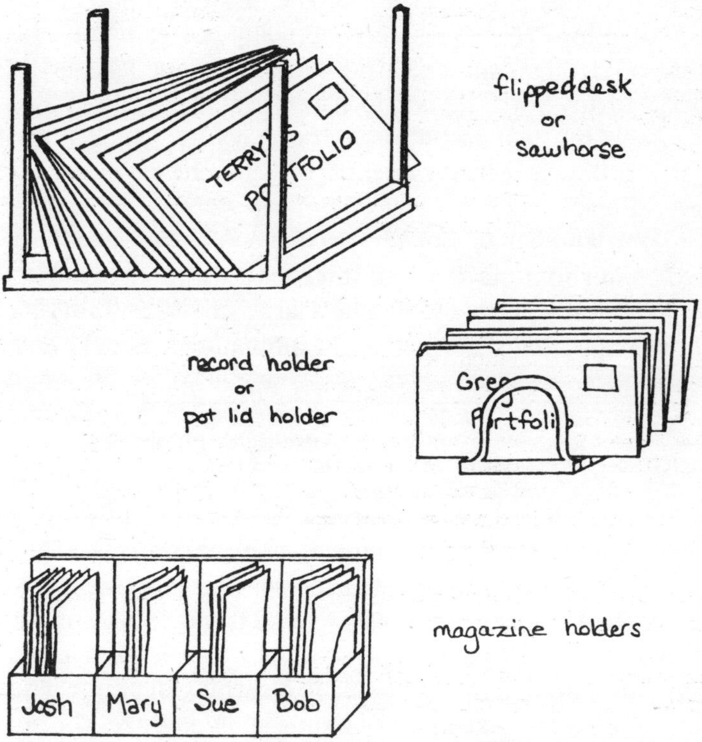

Hole-punching and using wool to "stitch" seams will make a portfolio more expandable and better able to hold more and larger materials.

• *Portfolio accessibility*

Take accessibility for teachers and students into account. If the portfolio is simply a tracking mechanism for the teacher, student accessibility does not matter. If, however, the portfolio is going to be used as a tracking and conferencing mechanism by both the teacher and students, both must have ready access to it. In this case, students must be able to manage the portfolio independently of the teacher, without disrupting the rest of the class.

• *The need for durability*

How durable the portfolio needs to be depends upon how heavily it will be used.

The portfolio's purpose affects this. If only the teacher is using the portfolio to track skills and student performance, less durability is required. Also, subject-specific portfolios, such as for mathematics, may not get used as frequently and would benefit just from lamination. However, a conferencing portfolio must be constructed of stronger material to handle daily use by student and teacher, and any portfolio intended to reflect the whole child should be extremely resilient and durable for heavy use. Such a portfolio may also follow a rotary student from class to class and be used by several teachers.

Consider whether or not the portfolio is grade specific or will be used throughout the division. If it has to last three or more years, it should not only be able to handle a large variety and varying sizes of work samples but be very strong. Laminating will make any portfolio stronger.

Developing Focused Assessment Tools

Teachers and students should work together to identify the learning outcomes to be assessed and the assessment strategies that would best reflect student mastery of those specific learning outcomes.

Rather than giving out the activity and trying to determine what learning has occurred, align instructional strategies and assessment and provide a predetermined focus for learning in your classroom. For example, a language arts outcome such as "uses the conventions of language" translates in a Grade 2 classroom into "uses capitals and periods." You could clearly focus on this by giving students a passage without capitals and periods and having them circle the letters that should be capitals and insert the periods. Recopying sentences from a blackboard, putting in capitals and periods would assess this, too, but would also involve copying, penmanship, fine-motor skills, none of which were the focus for the activity.

An assessment tool should readily demonstrate the child's ability. Questions that teachers need to ask themselves before they begin any instructional activity are, "Why am I doing this? What results do I want to see? What will the learning look like? Is this the best way of assessing the students' mastery of the knowledge, skill or attitude taught in the lesson?" For example, when teaching problem solving to students, you can best assess students' learning through reflection and discussion, not just evaluation of the end product. In this case process is more important than product — the assessment becomes a planned part of the ongoing lesson format. Teacher and students alike will find the learning more focused.

The activities or strategies used should represent all multiple intelligences. That allows students to demonstrate their strengths, as well as work on identified areas for improved learning.

> The theory of multiple intelligences makes things a little simpler for us. By chunking the broad range of human abilities into seven basic intelligences, we now have a map for making sense out of the many ways in which children learn and a blueprint for ensuring their success in school and in life.
>
> — Thomas Armstrong, "Multiple Intelligences: Seven Ways to Approach Curriculum," *Educational Leadership*, November 1994

Although teachers are required to teach specific curriculum to all students in a class, we understand that each child is unique. Students in a class represent many developmental levels. Ideally all children will be at the same level by a certain age and grade, but we realize that this won't happen. We must take these differences into account when developing plans.

Sometimes, the assessments chosen need to allow for some flexibility and choice on the part of the student.

> In our class, the topic for learning was research skills. As a class, the children decided the topic would be dinosaurs. Together, the criteria for success were determined, but the format of information delivery was decided by the individual students, suited to their learning styles. Some chose oral reports, others a poster, a pamphlet, a booklet, a diorama or a model. Susan was unique in that her strength was in fiction writing, and her project reflected that strength. She wrote a story that was fiction, but that contained all of the essentials to meet the criteria successfully. Susan had all of the research embedded in a fairy-tale like story. In this case, all of the students determined their own assessment tool, specific to their own learning style.
>
> — A Teacher

Although we encourage students to recognize and use their preferred learning styles, we also recognize that children need exposure to a variety of activities that reflect the range of learning styles. Providing this will enhance student learning, by allowing them to develop in other areas.

> The curriculum inevitably shrinks to the boundaries of evaluation; if your evaluation is narrow and mechanical, that is what your curriculum will be.
>
> — Walter Loban in *Junior OAIP Language Arts*

Using a variety of assessment tools appropriate to the student's development and level of achievement will permit a more accurate assessment. The following list provides some examples of assessment tools for use in portfolios:

- ***Checklists and observation guides***
  easy for teachers to use; covering specific details; permitting focused observation
- ***Informal inventories and surveys***
  little teacher time invested; whole class at once; attitudinal, knowledge or skill based
- ***Anecdotals/teacher observations***
  personal evidence pertaining to students; more details than just a mark or letter grade; contexts for other information
- ***Workfolders and profiles***
  provide a wide range of samples; show growth over time; provide a well-rounded picture of the child
- ***Project work***
  focus on the process and the final product; individual and cooperative group work; organizational skills (in terms of time, materials and format), research skills and presentation skills
- ***Audio and video recording***
  evidence of learning otherwise not captured
- ***Conferences***
  student ownership, feedback and responsibility; individualized; forums for setting goals and making plans for improvement; opportunities for students to become aware of their own learning; times to communicate about learning
- ***Student self-evaluation***
  essential to growth and monitoring of learning; gain of knowledge of their own strengths and areas for improvement

- ***Peer evaluation***
  feedback in a non-threatening context; a help with self-reflection
- ***Standardized tests***
  a basis for curriculum improvement; a way to gain insights that could be shared through a portfolio, test scores not to be included; "snapshots" in time; possibly not relevant to your students or program; reflections of how your children are doing in comparison to others
- ***Performance assessments***
  relevant, purposeful and real-life connections; focused on application of knowledge
- ***Selected response tests*** (T/F, matching, multiple choice, essays)
  allow you to design the instrument to suit the criteria; give you a variety of items to choose from
- ***Oral questions*** (Recorded audio tape — teacher questions and student responses)
  allow students who have difficulty with written answers to be evaluated fairly; allow you to probe deeply through questioning techniques; allow you to see how children think; enable students to clarify their thoughts by explaining why they chose the work sample

Regular and consistent recording of information from several assessment tools will provide teachers with information about student growth. They can therefore better direct classroom programming.

Observation is one important assessment tool. It, too, must be focused, purposeful and used to guide instruction.

You can gain clues to student learning by observing students during free time. Their choice of activity can provide insights into their interests, concerns and needs which you will find helpful when talking with students and helping them to develop their goals. Your observations can help you structure the program to best meet individual needs.

Student mannerisms and behaviors provide teachers with additional information on how to structure the program to support students. As an example, Joey's previous teachers had always required that he sit quietly in his desk in a row. It was a physical impossibility for this child to do so. Once Joey was told he could choose where to work, the quality of his work improved tremendously.

Teachers can gather other information as they observe students in a variety of situations. You may glean and record valuable insights as students engage in dialogues with their peers, problem-solving activities, brainstorming, drama, music, songs, and computer work, and as you review writing samples from different stages of the writing process. All of this will inform your discussions with them about their portfolios and improve teaching decisions.

Articulating Assessments

Once you have designed a task that will demonstrate the learning, you need to communicate your expectations to students using rubrics, exemplars and previously completed work. That way, students can actively compare what they have done recently, what they are doing now, and what the expectation is for the future.

Share the criteria with the students and encourage them to articulate what they are learning and which piece of work best demonstrates that. During a Student-Led Conference at the primary level, one pilot teacher found that the sharing and discussion of work samples took only a few minutes. The student was unable to explain to his parents what the samples represented and why they were chosen — the discussion was superficial only. This first interview pointed out to the teacher areas for improvement, one of which was to spend more time talking with students about work samples and criteria.

In order to help students communicate that information to parents, think about having the information in a written form. You might have the criteria typed onto labels which students can attach to the backs of appropriate pieces of work. The labels can be produced by a computer program. Or, attach a duplicated sheet to the work on which students can explain the selection and criteria addressed.

In any classroom, criteria should be presented in language that the students can understand and posted where they can see them. This easy visibility means that students can refer to the criteria frequently, which will refocus them on what they are supposed to be learning. The criteria may be determined by a district or a board; in some cases, through collaboration and discussion between teacher and student. The criteria for assignments, along with appropriate exemplars and rubrics, should be shared at the outset.

In order to help the students clearly identify the reasons for their choices, you could provide sheets for the students to list the work samples and the corresponding criteria that they represent. These sheets can then become part of the agenda for the Student-Led Conference. The information on them will assist the child in conducting a conference.

You can help students greatly by ensuring that learning outcomes, teaching strategies and resources are all aligned with assessment and evaluation to support learning.

Collecting and Managing Work Samples

Work samples chosen for a portfolio should provide evidence of answers to these three questions:

- What can I do?
- How do I know?
- What do I need to work on?

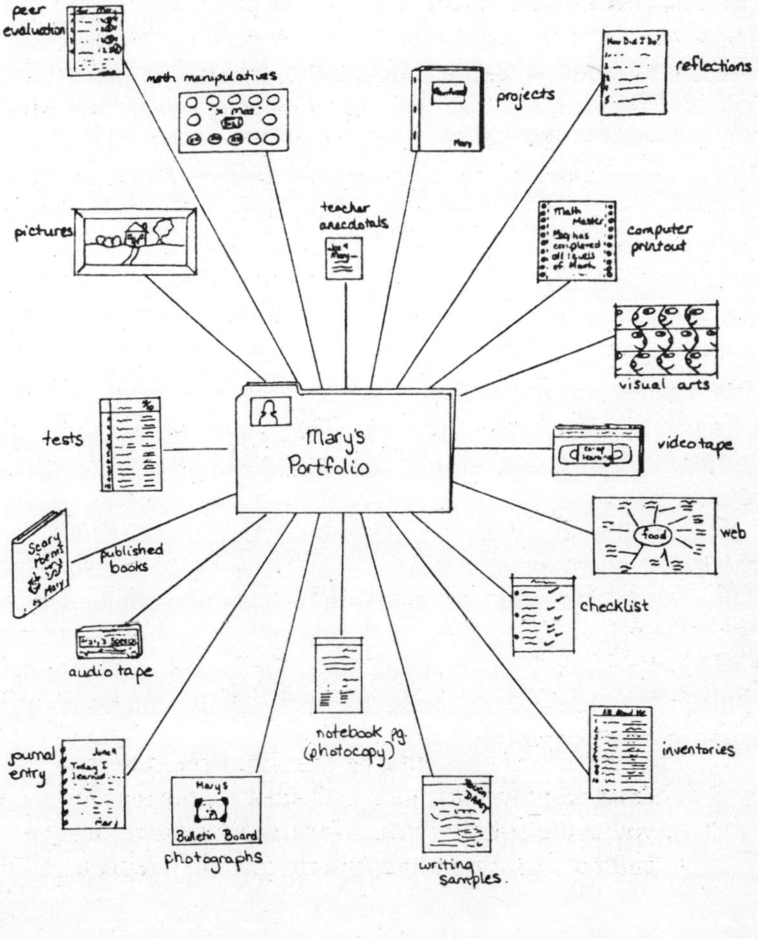

Students are responsible for collecting and managing the work samples. However, depending upon their age, the teacher may have to assume a more active role for a time. It is a physical impossibility for you to take the responsibility for a collection of work samples for the entire class. If you are collecting work weekly, it would probably take an hour per student to choose the work samples best representing student learning. In a class of 30, this could mean an additional 30 hours a week that would be better used on instruction and planning of the class program.

Students will need to understand the purpose behind collecting evidence of learning and have specific lessons on how to collect, choose and manage their work samples. You can encourage them to collect samples throughout the week, on an ongoing basis, and then select the work that best reflects their growth on a particular learning outcome. They can arrive at their decision alone, with a partner or with your input.

> A teacher in a Grade 1 classroom makes sure that at least once each day her students have a sample that they can include in their work folders. Every Friday at 3:00 p.m. the students go and get their work folders and spend some time deciding on which piece of work represents their best effort. They then share their sample with a peer, date-stamp it and file it in their portfolio to be shared with their parents at the conference.

The teacher may assign several pieces of work to provide evidence of a particular learning outcome. The student would then choose the best sample from among these, again with peer and/or teacher guidance.

Once collected, students will need to reflect on their samples and choose the best to date. (See page 72.) The best pieces, in turn, would demonstrate student achievement in relation to the intended learning. These choices, the frequency determined by you and the class, will be based on criteria that you and your students have identified. Students can use exemplars as the yardstick by which they should measure their performance.

Decide on how often you should meet with individual students to discuss their portfolio choices. A monthly conference with each student based on a significant body of work would provide a clear representation of students' abilities. In a dialogue between a student and teacher, the student can clarify and defend his or her choice of work samples.

Aim for a consensus about which pieces belong in the portfolio. If you can't reach one, however, make the final decision yourself. Consider what best reflects the whole child, the range of the curriculum, and the multiple intelligences at work. (See the list of possible portfolio pieces under "Developing Focused Assessment Tools.") The purpose is not to prepare for a one-time event but rather to show student growth over time.

Make the management of work samples an integral part of classroom life. You may initially see the time taken to select work samples and to reflect on the process as taking away from instructional time; however, the knowledge, skills and attitudes learned through the process represent the life skills curriculum that we should be teaching our children. Assessment is not an add-on, but a part of the curriculum; it promotes learning and student success. The time taken to do it represents an investment in children's futures.

> Pat Smith, a Grade 1 teacher at Maple Leaf Public School, has developed a three-part, folding portfolio the children in her class use with ease. It not only has made her job easier, but it has taught the children how to evaluate their own work, choose their best pieces and carry on a dialogue with the teacher about their learning. The organization is based on a tri-color scheme where yellow represents math, red represents language, and blue represents the arts and environmental studies. At the end of every day, time is set aside for the children to get their portfolios, which list the days of the week at the top of each section, and reflect on what has taken place that day. Pat simply focuses their attention on what the activities really meant using the color, for example, the snow pictures they made that day belong under the blue column. After deciding how they did on the task, the students would draw a symbol, such as a happy face, to represent their judgment. Periodically, the students bring their portfolios and meet with the teacher to discuss which pieces of work and which information can now be transferred to their individual portfolios.

PORTFOLIO CHOICE REFLECTIONS

Name: *Wojcziech*

1. I chose this work/product because *I like what I carved.*

2. I would like you to pay particular attention to *the head.*

3. One thing I would do differently next time is *take my time to do it.*

8: Reflecting on Learning

> The more thinking I did, the more I realized I could do anything.
>
> — A Student

The way to achieve our goal of empowering students to take responsibility for their own learning is through reflection. Reflection is the process of thinking about how you have learned, what you have produced and where you will go next. "I can see that I have reached the first two steps toward my goal. Now, I can work on the last step," wrote a student. If students can reflect on their own learning, they can better identify their own strengths and areas for growth. Turning to their portfolios for real evidence of what they have already learned, they can then set goals for future learning. They can critically analyse their own work in a meaningful way.

The time to reflect is before, during and after the learning experience. Ongoing reflection provides information for both students and teachers as to diagnostic assessment, formative assessment, and summative evaluation.

Students can reflect individually, but can gain additional information through peer reflections. Beyond the subjective opinion of a self-reflection, from only one perspective, they may benefit from constructive comments and/or suggestions from peers, to which they may be more receptive than they would be to comments from teachers or parents. Students tend to look critically at their own work, and may need help to see the strengths and gains they have made. Usually peers provide them with positive feedback. Conversely, children may have an unrealistic view of their accomplishments, and may benefit from a dose of reality from their more objective classmates.

Practising the Skill

Teachers can promote reflective learning with their students. Begin by talking with students about the purpose and importance of reflection and its relationship to their learning. Explain that their reflection will help anyone who views their portfolios to understand the criteria for their selections. They can think about and articulate the reasons behind individual choices. All of this will help them to consolidate what they have learned.

In order to fully understand it, students need to see the teacher model how to reflect. You may pose questions, think aloud, monitor yourself, and change something you do as a result. For example, if you discovered several students had difficulty spelling words with a particular diphthong, you could let students see how you go back and spend more time on that letter combination with them. As you reflect aloud, you make visible the process and illustrate the usefulness of reflection. Doing this allows students to see the significance of the reflective process for themselves.

Teachers must also let students talk about reflection in the classroom. As one pilot teacher said, "Setting aside two periods for reflection sheets wasn't helpful. It needed to be part of the program. It *is* the program." Move from whole-class lessons into smaller groups. To help guide an oral discussion, you might want to suggest questions similar to those about a science experiment below.

- Did the experiment turn out the way you expected it to? Why? Why not?
- Did you have the right equipment for the experiment? If not, what was needed?
- Tell me two science facts that you learned from the experiment today.
- How did your group work today? Did everyone have a role to play? Did they all fulfil the role?
- What problems did you have setting up or cleaning up your science experiment?
- What went well? What do we need to change?

Students could then work as a group, to solve identified problems and then make necessary changes to subsequent experiments. These questions could also form the basis of a written reflection.

If you are initiating students into the process of reflection, you may benefit from a very structured format. As time goes by individual needs or styles will probably play a larger role in determining the format used for reflection.

The type and complexity of the reflection instruments used depends upon the age and developmental level of the student. A primary class might use happy face stickers on a teacher-created worksheet to capture reflections, while older students may write in a learning log or journal. You can introduce reflection into the classroom in as simple a way as having children look at a story they have written and circle their favorite sentence. Can they explain their choice? Why is it their best or favorite sentence? Using the work samples provided in their work folder and given particular criteria, can they each choose the piece of work that best represents the criteria selected? Are they able to look at an early piece and a later piece and critique their progress? The more closely aligned the instrument is to a student's ability, the greater the depth to their reflections.

We have used a variety of reflection instruments. Three that have been completed by students follow. Each has been prepared before a Student-Led Conference and engages parents to some extent.

STUDENT SELF REFLECTIONS

Name: *Craig* Date: *Mar. 20*

1. This is what I have learned . . .
   — *I'm good at writing stories.*
   — *I have good ideas.*
   — *My spelling is great!*
   — *I need to work on my penmanship.*
2. I selected this piece of work because . . .
   — *my teacher sent it in for a contest so I know it shows I can write well.*
3. I want you to focus on . . .
   — *my descriptions and how the story makes you sad.*

STUDENT PRE-CONFERENCE REFLECTIONS

Name: *Tamara* Date: *Dec. 5*

1. What did I learn this term?
   I can multiply and divide big numbers.

2. What have I done really well?
   my number facts

3. I still need help with . . .
   subracting facts

4. I am really proud of . . .
   my board work in math

5. One goal that I would like to reach by next term is . . .
   to be the fastest at take-aways.

DEAR PARENTS

Date: *March 23, 1995*

Dear: *Mom & Dad*,

While you look at my work with me, I want you to notice these things about it. These are the things I do well.

1. *I put events in the correct order when I write stories & I use a organizer*

2. *I can always think of a good title*

3. *I have really good ideas*

These are the things I am going to improve.

1. *Spelling*

2. *Paragraphs*

3.

Would you like to make a comment to me after you have seen my work? Please do so.

I didn't know that you could write such long stories. I will try to help you at home with your spelling.

There are many natural opportunities for students to reflect. They can talk individually with you about their research projects, explaining their inquiry. They can write in a learning log at the end of the day, identifying two things they have learned and asking two questions to further their learning. Perhaps they can articulate to others how they solved a problem or came to a conclusion. Can they talk with a partner about their work based on the focus for learning? We never really understand something until we discuss or explain it to another. Any opportunity for students to think and talk about their learning will support the reflective process.

LEARNING LOG

Date: ______________________

Subject: ______________________

Two things I learned today

____

____

How did I learn? (Pick one of the above.)

____

____

____

PROBLEM SOLVING REFLECTION

Date: ______________________

Subject: ______________________ Peer/Self (Circle One)

1. Identify the problem.

2. What problem-solving model will you use?

3. Steps to follow to solve problem.

4. Describe your solution.

5. What did you find difficult? What did you find easy?

6. Can you explain how you arrived at your answer?

Since self-reflection is a critical component of learning, it would seem natural to mandate it for all students. We all have intrapersonal intelligence, but not to the same degree. To assume that all students can reflect is unfair. We must teach them the skill, nurturing its development and respecting its fruits. "I learned that all the things that I wrote felt good to share," said one student. It will take time to develop, but once in place, reflection in the classroom will support learning.

Teacher Reflections

Teachers also need to reflect on an ongoing basis in the classroom. Often unaware of the process, we consider a lesson that has been taught, how it went, and what we would improve for the next lesson. If we don't take time to reflect, we stop growing as professionals and stop learning. Reflection provides the feedback that allows us to fine-tune the curriculum, teaching strategies and materials to best serve the needs of the individual students. As a result, it has an immediate and direct impact on class instruction and student learning.

> Teacher reflection is defined here as taking time on a regular basis to step back from the often overwhelming demands of everyday classroom life and considering, through writing and discussion, what is happening in one's classroom and why. As part of this reflective process, teachers have an opportunity to think about possible new directions for their teaching.
>
> — *Journal of Staff Development*, Winter 1994

A powerful form of reflection occurs when small groups of educators engage in dialogue with one another. The benefit is enhanced when participants use specific questioning skills to support the reflective process. Reflective questioning creates opportunities for individuals to reflect aloud, to be heard by one or more colleagues, and to be prompted, expanding and extending thinking. As teachers collaborate to investigate issues related to teaching, instruction and learning for children improve.

Reflection that occurs before, during and after conferencing provides the teacher with feedback on what worked well and on what needs improvement in the process of conferencing. The reflective process aids teachers in understanding the nature of teaching and learning, knowledge that has a direct bearing on class instruction.

Parent Reflections

When we talk about Student-Led Conferences, reflection becomes equally important for students, parents and teachers. They all become partners in the process of learning.

Parents are responsible for helping to set the growth plan for their child, so they need to be involved, not on a superficial level, but on a deeper level where they can provide some insights into their child. They can come prepared with questions and recommendations, presenting their insights to their own child and providing valuable data about their child as a student. Reflection will better equip parents to help students set their growth plans and will contribute to more successful learning.

Encourage parents to reflect at home both before and after the conference. A reflection guide provided to them ahead of the conference would allow them to reflect on the upcoming conference and share any concerns about their child and his or her learning with you. You could then address any issues or concerns before the conference. The discussion at the conference would centre around the child's learning. Asking parents to respond at the time of the conference could cause some anxiety and would not likely provide a true reading of their feelings. The problem would probably be worse if English is not their first language. Parents need a chance to reflect in the comfort of home before responding.

The type of reflection tools for parents will vary according to their needs. It will depend upon their comfort level with the school environment, their previous experiences with conferencing, their facility with written language and what their first language is. You should probably start with a structured format which will elicit the information you need to improve the process as well as focus the parents' response. Some parents may require specific "sentence starters" in order to focus their thoughts. Other parents may appreciate a list of specific questions to address. Alternatively, you can provide some guiding questions for their reflective response. As they become more comfortable, the format can become more open-ended, such as an encouraging letter to the child shortly after the conference.

Two different reflection forms that parents have filled in follow.

PARENT RESPONSE TO THE STUDENT-LED CONFERENCE

Please tell me what happened in the conference. Did you like this kind of format? Did you feel comfortable? Did your child enjoy this kind of conference? Did you learn about your child's progress? Were they able to answer all your questions? Was there any aspect that you did not enjoy? Would you make any recommendations for the third term student-led conferences? Should we continue with this process of student-led conferences at Woodbridge Public School?

I would really appreciate you taking the time to answer these questions and any others that you might have regarding this project.

I feel the conference was successful. Format was different for a change. Yes, I learned about Lisa's progress from her directly which was a change. Yes, Lisa was answering our questions. I feel you should continue with this format; however, for some students who are a little shy, it could be a nervous experience. A little more coaching should be done.

Thank you Mrs. Landy and Lisa!

Name of student: *Lisa Lazovic*

Name of parent: *Maria and Peter Lazovic*

Signed *Peter Lazovic*

POST-CONFERENCE
PARENT REFLECTIONS

- What did you notice?
  Daniel is not very neat & erases too much.
- What made you feel proud?
  Daniel's original ideas & creativeness
- What would you like your child to work on?
  Handwriting esp. (slanting)
- Keep up the good work on . . .
  Math — multiplication etc.
- We/I know that sometimes you have difficulty . . . but . . .
  at least you make an effort!
- We are/I am glad that you are . . .
  participating & listening
- We are/I am glad that you are making an effort in . . .
  all aspects of school curriculum
- We/I can help you . . .
  Achieve the highest in all areas of school work!

Carol DeSousa
Mar 27/95

These both guide parent responses, with one offering critical comment to the teacher. Such reflections provide valuable information about parents' involvement in the conference process and the process itself. They help to validate the process, celebrate the learning, and bring closure to the reporting period. They also serve to reinforce children's self-esteem and confidence.

Both students and teachers need feedback on the conferencing process. Both parent letters or responses to students and parent comments in a guest book provided at the conferences will add another dimension to conference reflections. All participants should react to and reflect on their conference experiences.

9: In the Thick of Conferencing

I was really nervous, but once I got into it, I loved the feeling of power.

— A Student

A successful conference depends on much organizational work over a period of several months, all of which should be seen as part of the ongoing class program. Gaining administrative support, presenting a parent orientation meeting, booking a conference time which does not conflict with other school activities, preparing a planning calendar then following through on it with sequenced skill lessons that allow students to practise and reflect, practising conferencing, and discussing criteria and portfolio pieces with individual students all take place in advance. At the end of this, students should be able to articulate their choices of the learning that is represented and the significance of that learning.

Conference Scheduling

Timing during parent conferences is always a sensitive issue, and yet is critical to the event's success. As teachers we have all dealt with parents going over their allotted time and not drawing conclusions to their discussions. If one conference is late, it has an impact on all of the others. In some cases, where conflict has arisen and no agreement can be reached at the time, some distance may be needed for both parties to come to a comfortable resolution. In both these instances, an outside timekeeper to monitor conference times is an advantage. You can ask an older student, for example,

Grade 8, to act as a door monitor. Provide such students with the conference schedule you have devised ahead of time and encourage them to inform parents confidently that their time has elapsed. Giving schedules to the principal and head secretary also makes any phone calls or last-minute changes to the schedule smoother.

CONFERENCE SCHEDULE RM 5

TIME	TABLE A	TABLE B	TABLE C	TABLE D
4:00-4:30	Browns	Smiths	Bennetts	Andersons
4:30-5:00	Blocks	Adams	Aterninos	Azzarellos
5:00-5:30	Blythes	Drapers	Fiores	Fullons
5:30-6:00	Hasletts	Hathaways	Hyuns	Keays
6:00-6:30	MacDonalds	Mohammed	Perezs	Ramers
6:30-7:00	Rivers	Stahls	Wiltons	Edwards
7:00-7:30	Spallas	Pratts	Mercers	Gilroys

Rm 5.

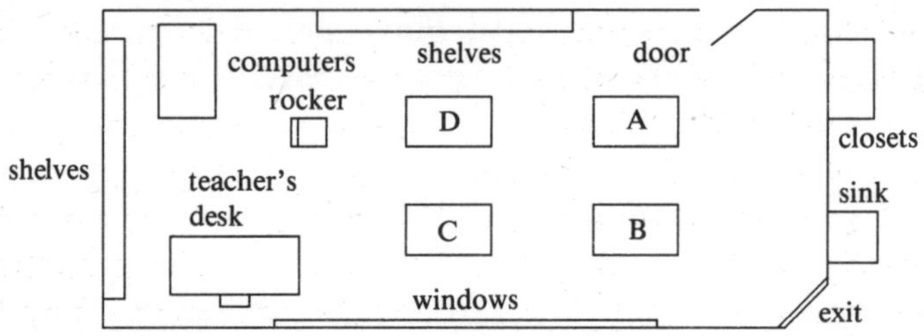

Refreshments will be served in the library.

If a parent cannot attend and can't reschedule, make sure that another adult is available for that student. In some cases, parents just can't make the conference, but are willing to reschedule outside of your selected conference period. If at all possible, try to accommodate the parents' request, as this is a way to gain their support and involvement. In one pilot school, a parent requested that the conference be rescheduled two weeks later. The teacher agreed to the change, the conference was held and the parent greatly appreciated the effort taken. "The parent saw that we really did care about the student's learning," said the teacher. Alternatively, the conference materials can be sent home for the student to gain the parents' contribution to their Student-Led Conference.

Plan to schedule every student who plans to share a video or audio tape with parents into the same centre. Remember to book equipment well in advance to ensure availability for the conferences.

Send the invitations home for the conference one or two weeks in advance. Although you would have informed parents of the date at the orientation meeting, send a written reminder, preferably in the language the parents prefer to use. Once you have received the replies, you can then start setting up your schedule. Expect revisions as last-minute conflicts arise with parent schedules. Depending upon the type of conference planned, you may need a translator/interpreter. If students are not fluent in their parents' first language, either the board or district, or the parent should try to provide an interpreter.

It is inappropriate for younger siblings to be present at a Student-Led Conference. If another sibling is there the parent will likely get distracted from the conference proceedings. Celebrating the student's learning remains the focus of the conference.

Parents cannot always arrange for child care, however. Perhaps students, if they are in Grade 6 or above, can take on the added responsibility of organizing and providing it. Older students in the school, members of the school's parent-teacher association, even a teacher's aide might provide this service. Alternatively, you may want to contact St. John Ambulance or a similar organization, which provides training for students in babysitting: at the completion of a specified number of hours, students receive a certificate stating that they have successfully completed the course, including a first-aid component. Aim to get all services provided for free. Perhaps you could arrange for the babysitting to take place in a gym, library, or another classroom. You want to make it as easy as possible for parents to participate.

An Inviting Environment

Providing a refreshment centre in the library contributes much to an atmosphere of celebration. It gives the children an opportunity to play hosts to their parents and lets parents relax and enjoy being with their children. The library, with all its resources and the potential for a book fair, is an ideal setting. Even if parents have to move on to another conference within the school or to another commitment right after a conference, knowing that the centre has been set up will help them appreciate the value put on the conferences.

Students will make many decisions as they set up the centre. They will have to determine what will be served, what quantities will be needed, what dishes will be needed, who is going to serve, where will the food be served, and how the centre will be decorated.

Students can raise money to establish their refreshment centre, thereby learning in a real-life context. Perhaps they can hold a bake sale, sell popsicles or popcorn at recess, or approach the school's parent-teacher association for a donation. If they don't want to raise the money in these ways, students may ask parents to donate the necessary ingredients for baking the refreshments, which they can make in advance and freeze. Or, they may choose to persuade parents to donate baked goods.

You will have to coordinate your classroom's needs with those of any other classes that have adopted Student-Led Conferencing. Perhaps you can bring the microwave oven from the staffroom to your classroom to do the baking. Doing this would eliminate the problem of supervising students in two rooms at one time. If you have access to a home economics/family studies classroom, try to make use of its facilities. Or, students can always buy ready-made baked goods.

If the school librarian has any reservations about the serving of food, and even if not, make arrangements for a couple of older students from the school to monitor the refreshment centre, replenishing supplies and mopping up any spills. That should reassure the librarian.

Ask students to design a class guest book to keep a record of those in attendance. Have them include a section for parents to comment on the conference for the whole class and/or to schedule an interview time with the teacher to discuss more personal concerns. This guest book should be left at the refreshment centre.

Students can make signs to direct parents to the conference site. They can make these signs from bristol board or fluorescent paper, using poster paints, markers or pastels. If the children have access to a computer, they can produce an effective computer banner, perhaps printed with a color printer. Encourage creativity.

The paper support you offer also helps to make parents feel welcomed. They may find reflection sheets and agendas, with generic ones sent home prior to the conferences, very helpful. These will vary depending on their experience as conference participants and their children's age, but all should be run off well in advance.

Conference Day

Many preparations can be made ahead of time, but several things must wait till the day of the conference. Students and teacher can work together to do them.

Have students post a welcome sign on the front door of the school directing parents to the classroom. Make sure that the door monitor is prepared. Is the student's desk set up? Does she or he have a conference schedule? This student will need to set up a few chairs in the hall and perhaps display some class books for parents who arrive early. A large schedule of conference times on the classroom door will help remind those involved that time management is important to the conferences' success.

Rearrange the furniture into group settings to accommodate the number of conferences scheduled for one time. Four centres seem to be most manageable. More than that may result in a very distracting noise level and raise concerns about confidentiality. For each conference centre make chair sizes uniform and provide a table to display student work. These groupings should be spaced to provide a comfortable setting and as much privacy as possible, while still allowing ample room for you to move around the room and interact where necessary. Make sure that the students have their portfolios close to their designated conference areas. Leave out additional copies of the generic agendas sent home for those who arrive without it, to give structure to the conference. Make sure that students have their personal agendas ready for their conferences. This agenda will guide both students and parents through the process comfortably and easily.

Let each student decide whether or not he or she wants a final rehearsal or practice on conference day. Those students who are anxious may need extra encouragement and would benefit from a final runthrough of the conference. But for some children a last-minute rehearsal would simply increase anxiety. The children themselves will know best whether or not a rehearsal is needed. Respect the individual needs of the students and provide time during the day to accommodate those students, as necessary.

Check for any last-minute problems, scheduling conflicts or absenteeism of both students and parents. These will affect the schedule and running of the conferences. To deal with any last-minute changes in parental plans, inform the individuals who have volunteered to fill in as "parents" for student conferences that they

MY PERSONAL CONFERENCE AGENDA

Name: ____________________ Date: ____________________

1. Introduction
2. Classroom Tour
3. Portfolio Sharing:

Work Sample | Criteria for Selection

1. ____
2. ____
3. ____
4. ____
5. ____
6. ____

4. Growth Plan — attached sheet
5. Refreshments

will be needed. Ensure that necessary materials and equipment are in the classroom, accessible and functioning.

Make sure that the refreshments are set up in the library and that the supervising students are on duty. Final considerations for the refreshment centre include putting the decorations out, setting up the table, tablecloths, and utensils, making coffee, and setting out juice.

Ensure that the babysitting area is ready with activities and materials. The supervisors should have a sign in/out sheet for parents, and be ready to greet children and introduce them to prepared activities.

Anticipating possible problems in advance will help you to deal with surprises: parents that don't show up, AV equipment that is broken, refreshments that have been eaten, or a coffee urn that doesn't work are all possibilities of what can happen! With luck, you won't have all these problems at once . . .

From her vantage point at the back of the room, the teacher could observe and monitor the dynamics of the four conferences taking place.

The teacher was delighted to hear one of the conferences being conducted mainly in Cantonese. Even though she was unfamiliar with the language, she could tell that the child was conducting the conference as planned, because he was following his agenda, sharing his work and receiving obviously complimentary comments from his parents. "Mom, I'm in charge of the interview. If you have any questions, just ask me," said the ESL student in English at the very beginning of the conference.

The second conference consisted of a single parent and child sharing strategies for improving the child's ability in math computation. "I understand that you now know how to do this," said the mother. "We can practise on speed at home."

In the third conference, a mother and father were complimenting their child on her improvement in reading, even though the reading level continued to be below grade level. They were overheard to ask probing questions to determine exactly where they should help. "What does this tell me about your reading? How do you know that's what the author meant?"

The fourth conference featured a mother and father negotiating with their child the components of the growth plan and what each would contribute to achieving the goals. "I can see how much you have improved since the last conference. What are you going to work on now? How can we help you?"

As the teacher monitored the conferences, she overheard other comments such as these: "We are glad you are working so hard." "I didn't know you could do that!" "I have learned so much about what you can do." "You are much more confident in this conference." "I noticed that you have improved in the way that you are writing, clearly and neatly." "I am capable of doing more things now," said a student.

As each group approached the end of the conference, the teacher drew closer, offering the student positive comments. "I am really pleased to see the growth plan you have developed based on work in class, and your parents' ideas. Well done, I think this is a good plan. Congratulations!"

This picture shows how even though each conference unfolds along a predetermined sequence, it is unique in composition and interaction. But all celebrate the students' learning.

The student is very much in charge. The following checklist, which your students may find useful, reflects that.

STUDENT-LED CONFERENCE CHECKLIST

_______ 1. Greet your parent(s) at the door and introduce them to your teacher.

_______ 2. Tour your classroom.

_______ 3. Perform in one of these ways for your parent(s):

- _______ Read a part of your favorite book.
- _______ Play a spelling game.
- _______ Do a math activity. Can your parents do it?
- _______ Play a game on the computer.
- _______ Conduct a science experiment.

_______ 4. Share your best work and explain why you chose it.

_______ 5. Tell/show your parent(s) what you are good at.

_______ 6. Ask your parent(s) what they think you are good at.

_______ 7. Write down what you are going to work on next term.

_______ 8. Ask your parent(s) how they will help you.

_______ 9. Write down your two new goals.

_______ 10. Give your parent(s) the form for the letter they are going to send you (if they wish to follow it).

_______ 11. Have your parent(s) sign the guest book and share the refreshments.

_______ 12. Thank your parents for coming and looking at your work.

10: Goal Setting

> It's about us!
>
> — A Student

Conferencing enables participants to find out where the students have been, where they are now, and where they are going in their learning. When they share their portfolios, students say where they have been. Then students and parents can celebrate where they are now. Finally, they can work together to finalize goals to show there the students want to go and outline objectives to realize them.

> For a Grade 3 student, the long-term goal may be to do multiplication better by the end of the year, the medium-term goal may be to know up to the five times table by the end of first term, while one short-term goal could be to know the two times table by the end of the week.

The curriculum, or students and their needs, or a combination of both, may determine the goals. Working with a teacher, each student identifies the desired learning outcome and then breaks it down into discrete steps to allow for cumulative success. Peers may provide valuable input while the students are learning to set goals. "Setting goals was a lot easier when my friend helped me," said one. The ultimate aim is for students to set goals for themselves independently, but this challenge demands that students get support.

Guidance on Goal Setting

Students do not enter the goal-setting phase of a Student-Led Conference cold. They will have had previous conversations with the teacher and indeed have gained ample direction in order to be able to set realistic goals, strategies and the timelines for achieving them.

They need guidance to recognize what they already know and to identify what they need to know. Setting unrealistic goals is common among students. They often expect to accomplish what's impossible given time restrictions or their own abilities. A child in Grade 1 who sets a goal to learn his multiplication tables as an older sibling has done would probably be setting an unrealistic goal. Indeed, this type of goal would be inappropriate for most Grade 1 children. Similarly, the child in a Grade 5 class who does not yet understand the concept of multiplication should set a goal to accomplish this.

Teachers must teach and model goal setting throughout the classroom program. You should provide students with much opportunity to identify goals with both you and student peers. Students can also work together toward achieving the goals.

The nature of goal setting and the approach to it differ between Student-Led and Three-Way conferences.

In the Student-Led Conference, much advance discussion and goal setting will help the student to prepare for the conference. The student, coming with partially completed goal setting and growth planning sheets, discusses learning and strategies for reaching identified goals with the parents. As the partners do this, their roles and responsibilities in meeting the goals will become clear. They play a significant decision-making role within a realm previously defined by the teacher and student. As the conference draws to a conclusion, the teacher *may* enter it to sign the growth plan and thank the parents for coming.

In the Three-Way Conference, the teacher and student will have previously considered aspects of goal setting and growth planning, too. Once at the conference, mainly the student and parents discuss outlined strengths and needs, and both predetermined and additional directions for future growth and goal setting. Near the end of the process, the teacher, who has been present throughout but who should avoid being treated by the parents as "the expert," actively enters the dialogue. The teacher has the role of drawing out and refining ideas discussed and acts as a facilitator as the student and parents complete the goal setting and a growth plan.

Students come to both types of student-involved conferences with a fairly well-developed sense of what their goals should be. Their parents validate and reinforce the goal setting, identifying ways in which they can best contribute to goal achievement.

Growth Plans

Goals that are realistic and attainable and that meet the individual needs of the student can be expressed as a growth, or action, plan. A **growth plan** is a form of written communication about student achievement, or possibly behavior, with about two clearly stated goals or outcomes and a focus for achieving them. It shows direction and responsibilities for all three partners — student, parents and teacher, whose contribution comes prior to the conference. It should be flexible with reasonable timelines and identify support strategies and appropriate resources. As one student said, "I knew what my goal was, but it was hard to come up with the steps to reach it." All partners participate in setting the plan as well as monitoring the student's progress.

The plan is treated as a binding agreement, a contract, with every participant signing. There should be three copies: one in the student portfolio so that the student can monitor his or her progress, one for the teacher's records, and one for the parents.

Once participants have agreed to a plan, they should establish a timeline for revisiting it and tracking progress. Much of this will be embedded in the steps for achieving a goal.

Goal setting is cyclical, subject to revision and tied to reporting structure, class needs, student progress and performance. The student, parents, and teacher may do it as a team three times a year.

Goal Monitoring

Teacher monitoring of student goals is feasible even for students on rotary timetables. Although each subject teacher will identify and monitor goals separately, either the homeroom teacher or a designated mentor teacher will need to check the overall plan. Care must be taken to provide holistic goals for all students so that they do not become overwhelmed by subject-specific goals.

As students begin to work on the steps leading to their goals, teachers may find that some of them experience difficulty. In this case, the teachers and students should revisit their growth plan, revising the goals and steps wherever necessary. Parents should then be informed of any resulting changes to the plan.

The following example is an outline of a written plan illustrating elements to be included. The growth plan is used as a vehicle for communication between the student, parents and teachers. It also serves as a method for documenting progress, and is summarized on the report card.

STUDENT GROWTH PLAN FOR ACHIEVING MASTERY

Student Lee Ann Michaels Teacher B. Brown Grade 4

Area(s) of Focus:
- Language Arts – spelling
- Mathematics – computations

Learning Outcomes Performance Criteria	*Action*	*Responsibility/ Resources*	*Timeline/ Progress*
1 *Language Arts Conventions*: knows and uses the basic conventions of language to communicate effectively • uses standard spelling for frequently used words	– 10 min./alternate evenings reviewing weekly spelling list – 20 min./alternate evenings playing spelling games – *McCracken* spelling program in class	– parents/ Lee Ann – *Scrabble* – *Boggle* – Ms. Brown	– improved success with high frequency words – recognizes errors in own writing – uses dictionary to check
2 *Mathematics Operations*: applies the knowledge of mathematical sense, systems and processes to perform real-life tasks • practises operations related to real situations: 3 digit addition and subtraction . . . adds/subtracts fractions with like denominators	– 10 min./reviewing math facts (tables up to 5 × 12) – 20 min. playing math games extra help at noon as needed Lee Ann asks for help in class when needed	– parents, Lee Ann – cards – *Reading, Writing & Rummy* (bk.) – *S'Math* – *Trivial Pursuit* (Math) – Ms. Brown – Ms. Brown	– able to × or ÷ up to 5 × 12 = 60

Lee Ann M.	*B. Brown*	*R. Michaels*	*Dec. 18/94*
Student's Signature	Teacher's Signature	Parent's Signature	Date

Review Date: *Mar. / 95*

SETTING GOALS

Subject: *Math* Name: *Nicole*

LONG TERM

By the end of the year I *will be able to multiply and divide quickly*

MEDIUM TERM

By the end of the term I *will be able to multiply up to 5 times*

SHORT TERM

By the end of this week/month (circled) I *will have memorize my times tables up to 5*

	Steps to Reach My Short Term Goal	What I'll Do to Reach My Goal ... At School	... At Home
1	*understand the 0 to 2 × tables* *memorize them* *know the rules and tricks*	*ask for help from teacher* *use × mats and counters* *use friends to help*	*dice games* *S'math game*
2	*understand and memorize 3 to 5 × tables and rules and tricks*	*× grid* *use calculator to check* *practise mad minute drills* *math games*	*Trivial Pursuit game* *card games*

SETTING GOALS

Dear *Mom & Dad*

I need to improve in the following areas:

1. *organize myself and my books*

2. *keeping my homework book up to date*

3. *division*

You can help me by *checking my book every night and reminding me about due dates and checking long ÷ questions.*

Taylor, I will be glad to help! Me too!

Signed *Taylor Cooke* *Mrs. Cooke* *J. L. Cooke*

Date *Dec. 8/94*

One of my Grade 3 students wanted to get his spelling perfect every week. He decided that the short-term goal would be perfect weekly dictations. Once I realized that he was having difficulty and that his goal was proving to be unrealistic, I sat down with him and completed a diagnostic assessment. This assessment identified gaps in his understanding of consonant blends. We set more appropriate goals and shared them with his parents.

— A Teacher

Provide opportunities for students to monitor their progress on a regular basis within the classroom program. One teacher uses the reading/writing workshop conference time as an umbrella under which she and her students discuss their progress toward their goals. Since students meet once a week for such conferences, they could provide weekly updates on their progress. At the same time, the teacher was able to identify those children who were not on track and could provide immediate redirection. Otherwise, students may give up on reaching their goals. Nothing succeeds like success.

If the goals are reasonable and attainable and the timelines appropriate, students should succeed in reaching them. If they don't, lack of commitment or interest may be the cause, but we haven't found this to be much of a problem. In this, as in all cases of monitoring goals, students should be held accountable for their actions, something that is easier to do when three parties, the students, the teacher, and the parents, are involved. Students know that they will have to explain and represent what they have done.

Conferencing as a Reporting Mechanism

Student-Led Conferencing can replace the written report card that has traditionally been sent home to parents. Legally, the administration within an area has some choice about reporting practices. For example, many Ontario schools report three or four times a year, because they have always done so. The growth plan generated by a conference could become the written record required by law.

All the characteristics of a good reporting process are true of Student-Led Conferencing and the growth plan that may accompany it. The ongoing process presents a picture of the whole child, provides opportunities for formal and informal communication, features positive, personalized information, calls for communication among teachers across subjects and grades, and is based on learning outcomes and performance criteria. Based on a common understanding of shared responsibility, it also provides suggestions for home support, self-assessment, and parent and student input. It includes a clear plan for student success.

Sometimes, a report card can enhance a conference. In that case, the teacher would have written it ahead of time and shared it with the parents and student. The conference then becomes a follow-up for the sharing of the information used to arrive at the conclusions stated in the report card.

Alternatively, the teacher can gather information from the conference to complete a report card/growth plan and share it with the student and parents shortly thereafter.

What is most true of Student-Led Conferencing, however, is to use the conference as the basis for reporting, with the sharing of work preceding the setting of goals for a growth plan. Here, the parents actively participate. Once the partners have finished goal setting, they all sign the growth plan and the parents can take away a copy of it with them.

Goal setting and growth planning provide form and direction for student learning and classroom teaching. As students become involved with both processes, they develop tremendous self-analysis skills and identify areas for focus and improvement. As parents become involved, they help to direct and support their children in a significant and meaningful way, listening and responding to their own children's needs and ambitions. For teachers, these two processes help to direct and drive the classroom program, ensuring that all partners in the learning team take responsibility for and get involved in the process of teaching and learning. Learning is the direct result of goal setting and growth planning.

11: Conference Aftermath

> When we saw what she could do, it brought tears to our eyes. We were so proud of her.
>
> — A Parent

Once all the conferences are over, hold debriefing sessions with the students. These class discussions should highlight what worked well, what problems arose, and what needs to be changed for the next round of conferences. Reflections on the conferencing process will yield invaluable information on how to improve the process itself.

Students should reflect on how well prepared they were to conduct the conference, how well they selected work samples, and how well they set realistic, attainable goals. They should also consider which part of the conference they found most difficult and conversely, which most easy. Once they have done this, they should work with their peers to address areas of concern.

If you and your students use a reflection log or journal, you can gain an ongoing record of the process. This would provide insights and directions for future conferences and learning in the classroom. It would also allow you to make adjustments to the process on an ongoing basis instead of waiting until the end.

Your reflection, taking into account student and parent feedback, forms the basis of the modifications you will put into place for the next round of conferences. You can work with your students to achieve these goals which can range from wanting to learn various skills by studying dinosaurs to overcoming shyness or lack of voice projection in a conference.

STUDENT-LED CONFERENCE NOVEMBER 30
BEFORE CONFERENCE

Dear Mrs. Landy

I am very pleased in coming in tonight for the conference. I am hoping to share all my work in Language Arts to my mom. I am a little nervous but I shouldn't be because I will be only talking to my mom. I hope that we can do this again soon.

Sean
O'Hara

STUDENT-LED CONFERENCE DECEMBER 1
AFTER CONFERENCE

Dear Mrs. Landy

I thought that the conference last night went good. It showed my mom exactly where I was in the L.A. program. It is also good to show your parents the work that you have done in school because not all the time do they get to see it.

I am looking forward to doing this again next term so I can show my parents my progress again in L.A. class.

Sean
O'Hara

Parents' Reviews

Ask parents to reflect on the conferencing process by writing a joint letter to their child. The personal nature of the reflection validates the child's learning and self-worth. To make parents more comfortable about reflecting, provide them with a reflection guide. They can use a format such as the following:

- Things I liked about your work . . .
- Things I was proud of . . .
- It was great to see . . .

Teachers should collect these letters. If any parents have not responded, remind them to do so. If, for some reason, a letter has still not been sent, provide a reflective one for the child yourself.

December 5, 1994

Dear Amanda,

Thank you for inviting us to review your work at your school. Your mother and I now have a better understanding of what you have been doing so far this year.

We are very pleased that you are doing so well in your school work. Your marks are certainly very good. It is important that you also enjoy doing your school activities. There is real reward when learning is fun.

Spend more time talking to us about why you are doing in school. We can take you places and show you things that will make what you are learning more interesting.

Keep up the good work, Amanda.

Love

Douglas G. Bernie *Fulvia Wilton-Bernie*

Dear Cody,

We wanted to take this opportunity to tell you how much we enjoyed the session in your Active and Healthy Living class during Parents' Night at Thornlea.

What struck us most was the confidence with which you presented your material to us. We were proud of the way you conducted yourself. Your review of your activities indicated to us that you are really enjoying this course.

We have noticed that since you started this course, you are more interested in cooking at home and are eager to learn to use the equipment, follow recipes etc. As well, it is not necessary to 'nag' quite as much about eating breakfast before you leave in the morning because you have developed an appreciation of the importance of this meal.

We hope that you continue to put into practice the information that you learn in Active and Healthy Living.

This will help you not only in school but in all aspects of your life now and as you get older. We hope that you continue to discuss aspects of the course at home as it causes our whole family to think about nutrition, exercise, eating habits etc.

We are glad to see that you are making an extra effort to stay on task and follow through with your activities.

We can help you by delegating more responsibility to you at home so that you have the opportunity to demonstrate your learning while carrying out household tasks ie. meal planning, cooking, shopping etc.

Keep up the good work, Cody. Be healthy always!

Love,

Dad and Mom

Cast Party

One way to acknowledge the amount of work that students have put into the process is to let students celebrate as a class. The children may have some suggestions about how to do this: a trip, a pizza lunch, a video and popcorn party, or class party. Keep expenses in mind! At this time, you could distribute the letters from the parents to the students. Doing so will let students enjoy a sense of satisfaction and bring closure to the process.

Ongoing Celebration

Then, the next day, the celebration of learning continues. Students are often thrilled by their conferencing and love to share personal feelings and anecdotes about what happened and what was said when they met with their parents. They can talk in pairs with peers to identify their learning and the meaningful feedback that they gained. Ask the students if there are particular comments from their parents that they are willing to share. Once they have done this, you can have a whole-class discussion to highlight recurring patterns and issues to be addressed. You can elicit solutions from the students.

Teachers should fully celebrate the learning that has occurred. You can create a celebratory bulletin board in the hall or the classroom, capturing responsive quotes and pictures of students in action during the conference and sharing their celebration with the rest of the school. You can record highlights not only in the school but in a district or board publication. Children can visit other classrooms that have expressed an interest in Student-Led Conferencing to share their positive experiences. The reason for celebrating is to validate the success of the experiences and to allow the students to give themselves a well-deserved "pat on the back."

Conclusion

We invite you to join our inquiry and experience first-hand the wonders of Student-Led Conferencing. Experiment with the suggestions in your own classroom situation and adapt them to suit the individual needs of your students, parents and school community. Once you see what happens in your classroom, we are confident that you will be amazed and committed to the process of Student-Led Conferencing. Student-Led Conferencing is an idea whose time has come!

Student-Led Conferencing celebrates student learning. It demands that students take responsibility for their learning and in so doing it promotes the creation of self-motivated learners capable of reflecting critically and constructively on that learning.

The process of Student-Led Conferencing empowers students. They play major roles in developing goals for personal growth plans and then must follow through and achieve those goals. Student-Led Conferencing supports students as they build a repertoire of skills they will need in any future learning situation.

This new type of conferencing also benefits parents in many ways. It gives them a significant role to play in their children's learning. They will thereby gain a better understanding of that learning and the school itself. It is also a more comfortable way for parents to discuss their children's progress; everyone knows what to expect and the conference can be conducted in the parents' first language.

Student-Led Conferencing provides parents with a forum in which to celebrate their children's learning. Today, once a child is past the toddler stage, how many times do parents say, "I'm really proud of you"? For many parents, the conference experience is highly emotional. The response letters they write to their children afterwards would bring tears to your eyes.

Student-Led Conferencing effectively engages parents in a meaningful level of involvement in the school and in their children's education. Once in place, it also makes your role as teacher easier. Because of the process, you, the parents, and the student become a learning team sharing responsibility for realizing the overall goal of school success for the student.

We feel teachers should implement Student-Led Conferencing: it makes students better learners and it gives them what they need to succeed, not only in school, but for life. After all, aren't two of the main goals of education to prepare students for their futures and to ensure that they have the skills to become lifelong learners?

Perhaps the main benefit of Student-Led Conferencing is that the students can take the skills they learn and the feeling of ownership that they assume outside the classroom. They can become lifelong learners ready to handle all the challenges of their future. What more can you hope to accomplish than that?

Bibliography

Armstrong, Thomas. "Multiple Intelligences: Seven Ways to Approach Curriculum." *Educational Leadership,* November 1994, vol. 52, pp. 26-28.

Armstrong, Thomas. *Multiple Intelligences in the Classroom.* Alexandria, VA: Association for Supervision and Curriculum Development, 1994.

Barth, Roland. *Improving Schools from Within.* San Francisco, CA: Joosey-Bass, 1991.

Beane, James A. "The Middle School: The Natural Home of Integrated Curriculum." *National Association of Secondary School Principals Bulletin,* November 1992, pp. 46-54.

Beane, James, Barbara Brodhagen, and Gary Weilbacher. "Living in the Future: An Experience with an Integrative Curriculum." *Dissemination Services on the Middle Grades,* June 1992, v. 23, no. 9, pp. 3-7.

Board of Education for the City of Etobicoke (Writing Committee). *Making the Grade: Evaluating Student Progress.* Scarborough, ON: Prentice-Hall Canada Inc., 1987.

British Columbia. Ministry of Education and Ministry Responsible for Multiculturalism and Human Rights. *Supporting Learning: Understanding and Assessing the Progress of Children in the Primary Program.* British Columbia, 1991.

Davies, Cameron, Politano and Gregory. *Together Is Better: Collaborative Assessment, Evaluation and Reporting*. Winnipeg, Manitoba: Peguis Publishers, 1992.

Faas, Larry A. *Children with Learning Problems: A Handbook for Teachers*. Boston, MA: Houghton Mifflin Co., 1980.

Ferguson, Ruth. "Involving Parents in a Culture of Co-operation." *FWTAO Newsletter,* Mar/April 1995, v. 13, no. 4, pp. 12-15.

Gardner, Howard. *Frames of Mind: The Theory of Multiple Intelligences*. Palatine, Illinois: Skylight Publishing Inc., 1991.

Grant, Janet Millar, Barbara Heffler, and Kadri Mereweather. "Student-Led Conferencing." *FWTAO Newsletter*, September/October 1994, pp. 22-23.

Grant, Janet Millar, Barbara Heffler, and Kadri Mereweather. "The Value of Student-Led Conferencing." *FWTAO Newsletter*. May/June 1995, pp. 38-41.

Hebert, Elizabeth A. "Portfolios Invite Reflection — from Students and Staff." *Educational Leadership,* May 1992, pp. 58-61.

High Success Network. *Student-Led Conferences K-8*. Colorado: High Success Network Inc., 1993.

Joyce, Bruce, James Wolf, and Emily Calhoun. *The Self-Renewing School*. Alexandria, VA: Association for Supervision and Curriculum Development, 1993.

Kiechel, Walter. "How we will work in the year 2000" in *Fortune* magazine, May 17, 1993, vol. 127, pp. 38-52.

Lazear, David. *Seven Ways of Teaching*. Palatine, Illinois: Skylight Publishing, 1991.

Little, A.W. (Nancy), and John Allan. "Student-Led Parent-Teacher Conferences." *Elementary School Guidance and Counseling*. February 1989, vol. 23, pp. 210-18.

Marshall, Kit, ed. "Student-Led Conferencing: A Four Star Winner!" *High Success Connection*. Colorado: High Success Network, April 1993, vol. 6, pp. 2-5.

Marzano, Robert J. *A Different Kind of Classroom: Teaching with Dimensions of Learning*. Alexandria, VA: Association for Supervision and Curriculum Development, 1992.

Marzano, Robert J., Debra Pickering, and Jay McTighe. *Assessing Student Outcomes*. Alexandria, VA: Association for Supervision and Curriculum Development, 1993.

Meisels, Samuel J. "Remaking Classroom Assessment with the Work Sampling System." *Young Children*, July 1993, pp. 34-40.

Ontario. Ministry of Education and Training. *The Common Curriculum Policies and Outcomes, Grades 1–9.* Toronto, 1995.

Ontario. Royal Commission on Learning. *For the Love of Learning.* Short Version. Toronto, ON: Queens Printer for Ontario, 1994.

Schlecty, Philip. *Schools for the 21st Century.* San Francisco, CA: Joosey-Bass, 1990.

Siegel, Janna, and Michael Shaughnessy. "Educating for Understanding: An Interview with Howard Gardner." *PHI Delta Kappan,* March 1994, pp. 563-66.

Sperling, Doris. "What's Worth an 'A'? Setting Standards Together." *Educational Leadership,* vol. 50, no. 9, pp. 73-75.

Stiggins, Richard J. *Student-Centered Classroom Assessment.* New York: Merrill, 1994.

Valencia, Sheila. "A portfolio approach to classroom reading assessment: The why's, what's, and how's." *The Reading Teacher.* January 1990, pp. 338-40.

Glossary

achievement: the demonstration of a student's learning at a precise moment in time

assessment: the ongoing collection of data about students or program

authentic assessment: a sub-set of performance assessment in which students demonstrate knowledge, skills and attitudes in a real-life situation

conference: a discussion with a clearly defined focus

criterion (criteria): a statement of a specific quality or characteristic which must be met

criterion-referenced evaluation: judgment of individual progress and/or achievement against a previously established standard

curriculum: a body of knowledge, skills and attitudes to be taught, mandated by a district, board or government

diagnostic assessment: evaluation done at the beginning of instruction to form the basis of planning

evaluation: a judgment based on assessment instruments in the form of a grade, level, standing or comment

exemplars: selected samples of student performance that illustrate the expected standard

formative assessment: evaluation designed to provide feedback to the student and teacher during the learning process. It is an ongoing, continuous assessment of both product and process.

grading: the practice of describing student achievement by assigning a letter or score

intermediate: a term to represent Grades 7 and 8
junior: a term to represent Grades 4 to 6
learning outcome: the knowledge, skills and attitudes that students are expected to acquire and develop. They are results oriented.
learning styles: natural learning abilities and preferences
multiple intelligences: identified by Howard Gardner as the "application of learning styles." The seven identified intelligences are Verbal/Linguistic, Logical/Mathematical, Visual/Spatial, Body/Kinesthetic, Musical/Rhythmic, Interpersonal, and Intrapersonal.
objective: a specific statement of intent within a particular program
peer assessment: a reflective practice in which students make observations about their peers' performance
performance assessment: an assessment in which students complete a genuine task (as opposed to a contrived one)
portfolio: a collection of work that highlights a student's abilities
primary: a term to represent Junior Kindergarten to Grade 3
reflection: the process of thinking about one's learning
reporting: communicating to students, parents and/or the community a summary of a student's progress and/or achievement
rubric: a rating scale of criteria or levels leading to the establishment of grades
self-assessment: a reflective practice in which students assess their progress in knowledge, skills, processes or attitudes
self-referenced evaluation: a judgment of individual progress and/or achievement against a previous evaluation of that same individual
standards: the points of reference which describe expected and accepted performance on critical learning outcomes by key stages in students' education
Student-Led Conferencing: the process whereby the student assumes an active role in planning, implementing, conducting and evaluating a conference with a parent. The teacher is not directly involved.
summative evaluation: evaluation designed to inform the student and teacher about the learning that has occurred at the end of a prescribed period of time, unit or theme
transition year student: a student in Grade 7, 8 or 9

Index

Blackline Masters

For Teacher Use

To be photocopied or adapted
and modified to meet your
needs in the classroom

JK-K CONFERENCE Date: ______________________

Participants: ______________________________________

PERSONAL CHARACTERISTICS:	
SOCIAL/EMOTIONAL DEVELOPMENT:	AREAS OF INTEREST:
LANGUAGE DEVELOPMENT:	PHYSICAL DEVELOPMENT:

READINESS SKILLS focus small-muscle control — pencil grip — use of scissors interest in printed material recognizes name, prints name, copies name picture-making interest in numbers/counting matching/sorting/creating sets one-to-one correspondence
Address: Telephone: Birthday:
PARENT'S COMMENTS:
CHILD'S COMMENTS:
GOALS:
SIGNATURES: STUDENT PARENT(S) TEACHER

REFLECTIONS ON CENTRE ACTIVITIES

Name: ____

ASSESSMENT FRAMEWORK FOR MEASURING STUDENT PERFORMANCE

Strand: ____________________ Grade: ____________________

Learning Outcome: ____

____

Performance Criteria: ____

Performance demonstrated	*Assessment rating*
	4 Demonstrating performance beyond expectations for grade
	3 Consistent demonstration of mastery at grade level
	2 Not yet consistent demonstration of mastery
	1 Beginning to work toward mastery

PORTFOLIO CHOICE REFLECTIONS

Name: ____

1. I chose this work/product because ______________________

____

____

____

____

2. I would like you to pay particular attention to ____________

____

____

____

____

____

3. One thing I would do differently next time is ____________

____

____

____

____

____

STUDENT SELF REFLECTIONS

Name: ____________________ Date: ____________________

1. This is what I have learned . . .

2. I selected this piece of work because . . .

3. I want you to focus on . . .

STUDENT PRE-CONFERENCE REFLECTIONS

Name: ______________________ Date: ____________

1. What did I learn this term?

2. What have I done really well?

3. I still need help with . . .

4. I am really proud of . . .

5. One goal that I would like to reach by next term is . . .

DEAR PARENTS

Date: ______________________

Dear: ______________________,

While you look at my work with me, I want you to notice these things about it. These are the things I do well.

1. ____

____

____

2. ____

____

____

3. ____

____

____

These are the things I am going to improve.

1. ____

____

____

2. ____

____

____

3. ____

____

____

Would you like to make a comment to me after you have seen my work? Please do so.

____

____

____

POST-CONFERENCE REFLECTION: PARENTS

1. Two things I am proud of my child for doing . . .

2. Two areas that could use improve . . .

3. Two things I would like my child to work on . . .

The following example is an outline of a written plan illustrating elements to be included. The growth plan is used as a vehicle for communication between the student, parents and teachers. It also serves as a method for documenting progress, and is summarized on the report card.

STUDENT GROWTH PLAN FOR ACHIEVING MASTERY

Student__________ Teacher__________ Grade__________

Area(s) of Focus:
- ____________________
- ____________________

Learning Outcomes Performance Criteria	*Action*	*Responsibility/ Resources*	*Timeline/ Progress*

__________ Student's Signature __________ Teacher's Signature __________ Parent's Signature __________ Date

Review Date: __________

SETTING GOALS

Subject: ____________________ Name: ____________________

LONG TERM

By the end of the year I ______________________________

____

MEDIUM TERM

By the end of the term I ______________________________

____

SHORT TERM

By the end of this week/month I ________________________

____

	Steps to Reach My Short Term Goal	What I'll Do to Reach My Goal ... At School	... At Home
1			
2			

SETTING GOALS

Dear ______________________

I need to improve in the following areas:

1. ____

____

____

____

2. ____

____

____

____

3. ____

____

____

____

____

You can help me by ______________________________________

____

____

____

____

Signed ____

Date ____